CW01496863

(All scriptures quoted in this book are from the following translations; King James (KJV), New King James (NKJV), New International (NIV), New American Standard (NASB))

I dedicate this book to my wife Debbie, who has heard the message of this book many many times, and has always encouraged me to preach it, and put it into print.

An Easy Guide To The End Times
(The Lost Treasury of Bible Prophecy)

Introduction

Our subtitle "The Lost Treasure of Bible Prophecy" is a fitting description both of this book, and my motivation to write it. I have always loved the subject of Eschatology, which I began studying as a teenager. Over subsequent years I have dug deeper into the subject with much intensity.

This research revealed to me a rich vein of Biblical understanding which has prepared me for what will shortly come upon this earth. Sadly what is coming will have terrible consequences for those who do not understand what is happening all around them right now, as we hurtle towards the ultimate destination of all mankind.

The treasure of verifiable end times knowledge has been lost to so many, and I long for people to hear these truths, perhaps for the first time, and to accurately evaluate the message for themselves. Today, we see people putting their trust in the slim hope offered by Mayan Prophecies, Nostradamus, et al, yet many of our forefathers had a much greater knowledge of this wonderful subject; all based on a solid Biblical perspective which could easily be verified and tested.

It is time for this vital message to be proclaimed again because now we can see everything lining up globally to usher in the soon return of the Messiah Himself, Jesus Christ, just as has been foretold in the pages of scripture.

My own life was impacted by the Bible's message back in 1975. I heard a presentation of the gospel, which, despite going to church regularly, I had never heard before. That powerful message completely changed me, and I developed a personal relationship with the God of the Bible, that has since been the bedrock of my life.

This relationship, rooted in Biblical truth, has seen me through many difficult times. I am privileged to have seen many miracles over these years (in my life and the lives of many others) and have proven God's promises in the Bible to be completely trustworthy in my experience.

In those early years I was blessed to hear some wonderfully inspiring sermons concerning the Second Coming of Jesus which shed such clear light upon my understanding and illuminated God's word so deeply, that they helped convince me that the Bible was true. Nothing has subsequently occurred to make me change my early opinion and especially now since events described so long ago in the Bible are being fulfilled right before our eyes today.

I hope this book will shine light on this vital subject and help you understand and trust the Bible, learn about the future, and most of all that you will come to know its author... God Himself!

Jonathan Fiddy

"I believe the Bible is the best gift God has ever given to man. All the good from the Saviour of the world is communicated through this book...All things desirable to men are contained in the Bible."

--Abraham Lincoln (1809-1865)
16th President of the United States

"There are more sure marks of authenticity in the Bible than in any other profane history."

-- Sir Isaac Newton (1642-1727)

CHAPTER 1

Why the Bible?

The first sign of the End of the Age I want to point to is the Bible itself. Its message centres on God's plan to restore man to relationship with Himself through the work of the Lord Jesus Christ. The ultimate outworking of that plan is the Bible's message as a whole, which points to the end of the age, and specifies all the other signs which we will look into.

Obviously as we look at the events concerning the end times we want to use the most reliable source available. I believe with absolute certainty that this is the Bible.

Why?

Well, the Bible has proved itself beyond any other book to have supernatural authorship, and to have been sourced from outside of the boundaries of time. Once established in this truth we can move forward knowing that we are dealing with sure and certain facts, and not wild predictions that may or may not take place.

The Bible contains knowledge which the writers could not have known about at the time. Let's look at some of this knowledge now...

Bible Knowledge

1. Man believed:

The general viewpoint of man was that the earth was flat. Even as late as the 15th century men feared they would sail off the edge of a flat earth.

Yet in 700BC the Bible said...

Isaiah 40:22 *"It is he that sitteth upon the circle of the earth"*

While it had hardly been considered, and far from being widely accepted, the Bible makes this definite statement that the earth is a sphere, risking its credibility. As always though, its integrity was subsequently proven by modern science.

2. Man believed:

During the time of Job man had various beliefs as to what held the earth in position. The ancient Egyptians believed the earth was held by a goddess and the Greeks that it was upheld by the god Atlas.

Job 26:7 *"... And hangeth the earth upon NOTHING"*

Job is the oldest book in the Bible! Written around 2000BC! How did Job know something that was not even thought of during his day?

3. Man believed:

Until the invention of the telescope there were only five thousand stars, those that could be seen with the naked eye. Ancient cultures had varying beliefs about the universe, but none had any idea of its vastness as the Bible lays out. Only in the 17th century did Galileo begin to see the enormity of the universe.

Jeremiah 33:22 *"As the hosts of the heavens cannot be numbered"*

Today scientists speak of vast numbers. The journal "Nature" recently published a study that estimated there were 300 sextillion stars. How did Jeremiah (605-582BC) know this, other than through divine revelation?

4. Man believed:

There was no knowledge of mountains under the sea until the 19th century, yet the Bible reads differently.

Jonah 2:6 (800-850BC)*"I went down to the moorings of the mountains."*

Jonah speaks of mountains in the sea, a fact only discovered by man in the last 100 years. Harold Leven in his book 'Contemporary Physical Geology' explains that oceanographers believed until recently that the ocean floors were flat plains. A lead weight on a rope was used to measure depths and those measurements taken led to this false belief.

The Bible also speaks of the currents. Matthew Maury who was a Bible believer was inspired to investigate by Psalm 8:8...

"And the fish of the sea, and whatsoever passeth through the paths of the seas."

He wrote a book in 1855 called 'The Physical Geography of the Sea and its Meteorology." He felt that if the Bible talked of paths in the sea they must exist and he began to investigate. As a result he discovered the currents system, and more besides, which proved the accuracy of Bible knowledge.

Incidentally Jonah is not the only one to be swallowed by a big fish and live. James Barclay had the same experience. He was swallowed by a Cachalot whale. A few days later the whale was caught and alive inside was James, bleached white!

5.   Man believed:

Man evolved from bacterial slime. David Attenborough claims the first life was single celled organisms, bacteria and archaea, which eventually evolved into multi cell organisms, and that life began to evolve from these. (See his website 'First Life' for more).

Genesis 2:7 *"And the Lord God made Adam from the dust of the ground."*

There are 28 base and trace elements in the human body, all contained in the dust of the ground. Today science agrees, the composition of the human body, and that all that was needed is indeed contained in the constituents of the ground (Please see The "Answers in Genesis" website for more details).

6. Man believed:

For centuries, in the main, people washed in standing water because they were ignorant of stagnant water holding disease yet the Bible teaches a better way.

Leviticus 15:13 *"... He must wash his clothes and bathe himself with fresh water, and he will be clean."*

Today we recognise the need to wash away germs with fresh water. When dealing with disease, clothes and body should be washed under running water. Even today the world health organisation estimates that 88% of all diarrhoeal disease is connected with contaminated water.

7.   Man believed:

No specific time to circumcise was necessary. There is no evidence of any other nation having a specific time to circumcise.

The Bible however gives explicit instructions that circumcision was to be done on the eighth day for vital health reasons.

Leviticus 12:3 *"And on the eighth day the flesh of his foreskin shall be circumcised."*

Now we know the clotting agent prothrombin (vitamin K) peaks on the eighth day. This is the safest day to circumcise a baby.

In 1935 Professor H Dam first proposed the anti-clotting agent was to be called Vitamin K. Holt and McIntosh, in their classic work, Holt Paediatrics, discovered babies are susceptible to bleeding from days two to five . Vitamin K is built from days five to seven, making the eighth day perfect.

There are many other subjects that the Bible shows knowledge of; for example Job records details of the hydrological water cycle, water evaporating, turning to cloud and becoming rain (Job 36:27-28). Leviticus tells us that life resides in the blood long before its nature was recognised by medical science (Leviticus 17:11).

This is just touching the surface of the knowledge the Bible contains that was light years before its time.

Hence, we can see that the Bible contains many examples that show it has knowledge outside of its time frame. These all point to its divine origin and therefore can be trusted.

The Life of Jesus told in Advance

The Bible not only has this knowledge in advance, it has also predicted future events long beforehand. While there are many examples of this in its pages, the most amazing is the fact that the birth, life, death and resurrection of Jesus Christ were foretold in the Old Testament.

Throughout the Old Testament predictions and references were made about the promised Messiah or King of Israel. Not only do these directly prove that Jesus Christ was the promised Messiah, but they also show that these predictions could not have been made by chance.

FC Payne in his book "The Seal of God" worked out the probabilities that Jesus was the Messiah and found it fulfilled the law of null probability. There are many other works which detail the amazing odds of these predictions being fulfilled including Chuck Missler's book "Through the Bible in 24 Hours."

The pre-dating of the Biblical texts is also beyond question, and in fact the Old Testament books were translated into the Greek "Septuagint" in 270BC.

Alexander the Great commissioned 70 scholars to translate the Old Testament (hence the name 'Septuagint'). The date of this is beyond question and for our purpose saves arguing over the dating of specific books.

It is incredible to think that hundreds of years before He was born, the birth, life, death, and resurrection of Jesus was a story already foretold. He was not the only person described and named before they were born, but we will centre our thoughts in this chapter on the Lord Jesus Christ.

There are around 300 prophecies in the Old Testament concerning Jesus' first coming that were all fulfilled. (It is interesting to note that prophecies concerning his second coming outnumber them eight to one by the way).

We are going to look at just a few of these; otherwise this chapter alone would fill a very large book! Just this shows beyond doubt that only someone outside of the restrictions of time could have inspired these verses. For one or two to be right could be chance. If just one were wrong it would raise serious questions. The facts are that they were all 100% accurate!

These predictions about Christ not only fully authenticate who He is, but by doing so fully validate his claim to be the promised one to the Jews (their Messiah), and also the only one who could answer the world's problems. Truly the promised "Saviour of the World."

No wonder Jesus said to the disciples...

Luke 24:25-27 *"O foolish ones, and slow of heart to believe in all that the prophets have spoken! Ought not the Christ to have suffered these things and enter into his glory? And beginning at Moses and all the prophets, he expounded to them in all the scriptures the things concerning himself."*

Let's look at the predictions shall we?

Prediction (700 yrs before fulfilment)

Micah 5:2 *"But you, Bethlehem Ephrathah, though you are little among the thousands of Judah, yet out of you shall come forth to me the one who shall be ruler in Israel, whose goings forth are from of old, from everlasting."*

Fulfilment

Matthew 2:1 *"Now when Jesus was born in Bethlehem of Judea in the days of Herod the king, behold, there came wise men from the east to Jerusalem."*

Messiah, the only one who could fit the above description (none other could claim to have an everlasting past) would be born in Bethlehem.

Prediction (725 years before fulfilment)

Hosea 11:1b *"And out of Egypt I called my son."*

Fulfilment

When Jesus had been born being warned by an angel Joseph and Mary fled to Egypt.

Matthew 2:14 *"When he arose, he took the young Child and His mother by night and departed for Egypt,"*

Moving on to the time of his betrayal...

Prediction (520 years before fulfilment)

Zechariah 11:12-13 *"And I said unto them, if ye think good, give me my price; and if not, forbear. So they weighed for my price thirty pieces of silver. 'And the Lord said to me throw it to the potter - that princely sum they set on me.' So I took the thirty pieces of silver and threw then in the house of the Lord for the Potter."*

Fulfilment

Matthew 26:15 *"And said unto them, what will ye give me, and I will deliver him unto you? And they covenanted with him for thirty pieces of silver."*

That's not all (we have INTENSE detail that follows...)

Continued Details

Matthew 27:6-7 *"And the chief priests took the silver pieces, and said it is not lawful to put them into the treasury, because it is the price of blood. And they took counsel, and bought with them the potter's field, to bury strangers in."*

Continued Fulfilment

Zechariah deals with the thirty pieces of silver, the price they put on Jesus to betray him, which in turn, 520 years later was exactly what Judas was paid to betray Jesus, and then Zechariah mentions it was used to buy the potter's field. Judas threw the money back to the chief priest, and the money was indeed used to buy the potter's field, a place for the burial of those of no means.

Isn't that amazing?!

This is certainly no conspiracy; had the Jewish leaders thought for one moment their actions were actually authenticating the Lord Jesus as Messiah they would have been mortified. They were the very ones who hated him, and arranged the crucifixion.

What amazing detail there is in just this one portion alone!

Prediction (1000 years before)

Psalm 41:9 *"Even my own trusted familiar friend who ate my bread has lifted up his heel against me"*

Fulfilment

In John 13:26 Jesus says *"'It is he to whom I shall give a piece of bread when I have dipped it' And having dipped the bread he gave it to Judas Iscariot."*

Prediction (1000 years before fulfilment)

Psalm 22:16 *"For dogs have compassed me: the assembly of the wicked have enclosed me: they pierced my hands and my feet."*

Fulfilment

This prophecy, clearly fulfilled in Jesus' crucifixion is remarkable as it was written long before crucifixion had even been invented as a method of execution.

Prediction (700 years before fulfilment)

Isaiah 50:6 *"I gave my back to the smiters, and my cheeks to them that plucked off the hair: I hid not my face from shame and spitting."*

Fulfilment

Mark 14:65 *"And some began to spit on him, and to cover his face, and to buffet him, and to say unto him, Prophesy: and the servants did strike him with the palms of their hands."*

The NIV is clearer...

"I offered my back to those who beat me, my cheeks to those who pulled out my beard; I did not hide my face from mocking and spitting"

Prediction (1000 years before)

Psalm 69:21 *"They gave me also gall for my meat; and in my thirst they gave me vinegar to drink."*

Fulfilment

John 19:29 *"Now there was set a vessel full of vinegar: and they filled a sponge with vinegar, and put it upon hyssop, and put it to his mouth."*

Prediction (1000 years before)

Psalm 22:8 *"He trusted on the lord that he would deliver him: let him deliver him, seeing he delighted in him."*

Fulfilment

Matthew 27:43 *"He trusted in God; let him deliver him now, if he will have him: for he said: I am the son of God."*

Prediction (1000 years before)

Psalm 34:20 *"He kept all his bones: not one of them is broken."*

Fulfilment

John 19:33 *"But when they came to Jesus, and saw that he was dead already, they break not his legs."*

Prediction (1000 years before fulfilment)

Psalm 22:18 *"They divide my garments among them, and for my clothing they cast lots."*

Fulfilment

Mark 15:24 *"And when they had crucified him, they parted his garments, casting lots upon them, what every man should take."*

Prediction (700 years before)

Isaiah 53:9 *"And he made his grave with the wicked, and with the rich in his death; because he had done no violence, neither was any deceit in his mouth."*

Fulfilment

Matthew 27:57-60 *"When the even was come, there came a rich man of Arimathaea, named Joseph, who also himself was Jesus' disciple: [58] He went to Pilate, and begged the body of Jesus. Then Pilate commanded the body to be delivered. [59] And when Joseph had taken the body, he wrapped it in a clean linen cloth, [60] And laid it in his own new tomb, which he had hewn out in the rock."*

These verses alone are enough to validate the Bible's message. There are no other examples outside of the Bible of such accurate information being given in advance in any other area of historical research.

Now let's look at how good humans are at predicting the future...

Predictive Failure

In fact man's attempts to predict the future, even the near future, have failed miserably.

Popular Mechanics, March 1949 said... *"Computers in the future may have only 1,000 vacuum tubes and weigh only 1.5 ton."*

The president of the Michigan Savings Bank said... *"The horse is here to stay, but the auto mobile is only a novelty—a fad."*

This was advice given to Henry Ford's lawyer Horace Rackham. Rackham wisely ignored this advice and invested $5000 in Ford stock, selling it later for $12.5 million.

British Parliamentary Committee, Commenting on Edison's light bulb, 1878 said... *"Good enough for our transatlantic friends... but unworthy of the attention of the practical or scientific."*

Hmm...

Margaret Thatcher on October 26th 1969 said... *"It will be years - not in my time, before a woman will become Prime Minister"*

The famous French thinker Voltaire in 1694-1778AD said... *"I will go through the forest of the scriptures and girdle all the trees, so that in one hundred years Christianity will be but a vanishing memory."*

Attempts at "prophecy" through the like of Nostradamus, almanacs and astrologers also prove to be vague and littered with errors.

Prophecies That Failed

Only a few of the predictions of Nostradamus were actually dated and therefore specific. Here are some clear predictions that all failed.

- The Roman church will conduct widespread persecutions of astrologers in 1607 (Quatrain 8–71)

- Arabs will capture the King of Morocco in 1607 (Quatrain 6–54)

- A monk from Campania will be elected Pope in 1609 (Quatrain 10–91)

- Turkey will subjugate vast areas of Europe in 1700 (Quatrain 1–49)

- The Turks will capture the King of Persia in 1727 (Quatrain 3–77)

- Upheavals of nature or famine will nearly destroy the human race in 1732

- There will be culmination of a long and savage religious persecution occurring in 1792 (Epistle)

- In the 7th month of the year 1999, from the sky will come a great King of Terror; to bring back to life the great King of the Mongols; before and after Mars to reign by good luck. (Quatrain10-72)

The name "King of Terror" has been considered, among other subjects, as the Antichrist, nuclear war, a giant meteor, and a solar eclipse.

Nothing happened from ANY of the above that can be considered a fulfilment.

There has been a lot of hype about the ending of the Mayan calendar in 2012. In fact there is no evidence this is of any prophetic significance at all, or that the Maya really believed it would signify the end of the world.

While the Maya knew some astronomy and did have the skill to predict eclipses, their belief system which included blood-letting and human sacrifice has little to suggest any superior insight or knowledge.

From psychics to seers, man will go on predicting the future. No doubt on occasions he will be right, but there is only one certainty in life worth basing prediction on. This is the word of God because it HAS ALREADY PROVEN ITSELF TO BE ACCURATE 100% of the time.

For most of us we would rather not know the future, leaving it in God's hands. The Bible is certainly not meant to be used as a way of fortune telling. However, as we read it, it becomes obvious that the Bible is not limited by the time domain, and that God who is the beginning and the end of all things inspired every word.

It is a book filled with astonishing detail. The most simple may understand its message, yet its depth is eternal. While we may have clear and certain details of coming events, we can be sure there is even more contained in its depths just waiting to be explored by every diligent student.

The Bible is very different to all other books; it lays its credibility on the line by making clear predictions. These as we have seen can be verified very easily.

Unity of the Writers

One amazing truth of the Bible is that despite being written over a 1500 year period, by 44 people from all different backgrounds, from Kings to shepherds to fishermen, it has an agreement of doctrine that is far beyond chance.

Even if all the writers had collaborated it would have been hard to keep the unity of teaching that is both implicit and explicit in the text.

For example, doctrines like the trinity, which appears from Genesis to Revelation. This doctrine was not even understood by the Jews at the time of the writing of the Old Testament, yet it is there in the text. This unity speaks of the fact that though many different people were used to write the Bible from many times, cultures and backgrounds, ultimately the author is God.

Many of these writers were not well educated, and did not know one another, yet great men through the ages have acknowledged that the Bible is one of the world's greatest pieces of literature.

Can you imagine giving forty authors, many not knowing the other, the job of writing a chapter of a book? There would be little chance of a masterpiece! No, the Bible's inspiration was from God!

What about copying?

One of the common objections to the Bible is that any book that has been copied over so many years cannot possibly be reliable.

Well...

When compared to other ancient documents, the Old Testament is astonishingly consistent. Professor Wilson's studies have shown that of forty Kings living from 200 to 400 BC each appears in chronological order. He concludes this is far from mere circumstance and that no stronger evidence of the substantial accuracy of the Old Testament records could be imagined.

As for the accuracy of transmission Atkinson, Under Librarian of Cambridge University says this feat alone is "little short of miraculous".

The scribes who copied the Bible gave their whole lives to the task, and would reject a document should there be even the smallest mistake such as the misspelling of just ONE word.

William Green (Old Testament scholar at Princeton Theological Seminary) says "It may safely be said that no other work of antiquity has been so accurately transmitted."

The New Testament has some documents dating back to just 100 years from the original. Both Old and New Testaments have been confirmed in their accuracy by archaeology and historical settings.

Ancient versions of the Old Testament used by missionaries in Syrian and Latin languages have been proven accurate. There are over 15,000 copies of these versions existing.

Comparing the Bible to other trusted ancient manuscripts shows a vast difference in favour of the Bible's accuracy. Few historians would question Caesar's "The Gallic Wars" yet there are only 10 ancient copies dating no closer than 1000 years from the original.

Homer's Iliad has 643 copies, yet with a 400 year time lapse. The New

Testament has 5366 fragments of scripture dating to 50 years, 200 books to 100 years and 325 complete new testaments dating to 225 years.

Furthermore, the New Testament is confirmed by other religious and secular writings of the time. Josh McDowell in his book "The New Evidence that Demands a Verdict" lists many, including...

Eusebius: In his Church History, Eusebius preserves the writings of Papias, Bishop of Hierapolis (AD 130), in which Papias records sayings of the apostle John.

Irenaeus: Irenaeus was Bishop of Lyons (AD 180) and student of Polycarp. Polycarp had been a disciple of the apostle John. Irenaeus wrote,

"So firm is the ground upon which the gospels rest, that the very heretics themselves bear witness to them, and, starting from these [documents], each one of them endeavours to establish his own particular doctrine."

Clement of Rome, Ignatius, Tacitus, Josephus, and the Talmud all provide evidence outside of the Bible itself.

In other words, the Bible is more reliable than other ancient texts and has shown itself to have been kept true to the original manuscripts over thousands of years.

The Bible has been protected

No book has been more questioned, abused, criticised and misused than the Bible. It has been banned, dismissed, even burned. The Roman Emperors banned it and sought to have it destroyed. The Communists went to great lengths to wipe out the Bible, and to destroy the faith of Christians. Even the church has in history tried to withhold the scriptures from the ordinary person in the pew. Yet despite all the opposition, the Bible has still sold more copies and been translated into more languages than any other book. Even today it is still a worldwide best-seller.

The words of Jesus are true.

Matthew 24:35 *"Heaven and earth shall pass away, but My words shall not pass away"*

Isaiah 40:8 *"The grass withereth, the flower fadeth: but the word of our God shall stand for ever."*

Perhaps the greatest attacks on the Bible's integrity have come from higher criticism via academics opposed to Christianity. This form of thinking took hold during the 19th century and said the Bible could not been taken literally and was full of errors. Large portions of the church were swayed by these arguments which gradually seeped into Christianity and now many Churches no longer accept the Bible as God's word, some even openly maligning its integrity themselves.

However, many of the supposed errors have been shown to be false as archaeology has uncovered more evidence of the past. Strangely these advances seem to have been ignored. It is sad that many in the pulpits of churches today do not themselves believe the Bible to be God's word.

One cannot pass this chapter without discussing the Theory of Evolution. Many books have been written on the subject, so here I just want to add a few thoughts. I am not a scientist and will therefore leave the intricacies for those that are.

The greatest evidence of Leonardo de Vinci is his great master pieces. I doubt that anyone would look at these works of art and not believe there was a great artist behind them.

Hence, the things that people create are evidence of their existence. As we look around at the incredible intricacy and design of nature it is inconceivable that there was not a creator behind it.

How can an egg bring forth a peacock? An egg that develops, hatches and every feather matches to produce a wonderful pattern in the new bird? An acorn grows and produces the magnificent oak. How can a small seed be programmed with the glory of a plant deep within itself unless a programmer had designed it so?

How does a bird know where to migrate to? The intricacies of life show there has to be some form of creator. On looking at a beautiful Swiss watch would you doubt for a minute there was a creator, would you consider it may have come together by chance? Maybe a big explosion at the watchmakers created it and it slowly evolved to become a beautiful watch.

How ridiculous!

Yet nature and man is far more intricate and complicated. No, I insist that there must be a creator, a master whose skill surpasses any other.

In fact...

God points man to view his handiwork as evidence enough of his existence...

Romans 1:20 *"For the invisible things of him from the creation of the world are clearly seen, being understood by the things that are made, even his eternal power and Godhead; so that they are without excuse."*

It is often said you cannot believe in science and evolution. However there are many, many scientists who do believe the biblical creation account.

Anne Lamont in her book "21 Scientists that Believed the Bible" looks at great names such as Newton, Kepler Faraday and Pasteur and their belief of the creation account. John H Ashton Phd in his book "In Six Days" presents accounts from fifty scientists that believe in a literal six day creation. Many scientists do not accept the theory of evolution.

It is sad that many publications and reports now cite all creationists as non-intellectual and tell us that all true intellectuals believe evolution. This is simply not true. In Romans, where the history of mankind is recorded it says...

Romans 1:22 *"Professing themselves to be wise, they became fools"*

So one way or another the Bible has withstood constant attacks but still remains. Ever since the Garden of Eden when Satan, the father of lies, questioned God's word to Adam and Eve he has continued to attack God's word in every conceivable way. This will continue as we come to the end of the age. It is his ultimate aim to close God's word and to stop people hearing the truth. Thank God that these words will remain forever, as yet another fulfilment of prophecy.

2 Corinthians 4:3-4 *"But if our gospel be hid, it is hid to them that are lost:In whom the god of this world hath blinded the minds of them which believe not, lest the light of the glorious gospel of Christ, who is the image of God, should shine unto them."*

Dr Ivan Panin

I cannot finish this chapter without a brief mention of the work of Dr Ivan Panin.

He was born in Russia December 12th 1885 and became a mathematical genius and a Harvard scholar. He was a firm agnostic.

In 1890 while reading the text of John 1:1 he was intrigued, and began to discover a previously hidden numerical pattern. He went on to devote the next 50 years of his life to this study and produced 40,000 pages of research.

In 1899 Panin sent a letter to the New York Sun challenging his audience to disprove his thesis that the numerical structure of scripture showed its divine origin.

He said "the laws of probability are exceeded into the billions when we try and rationalise the authorship of the Bible as the work of man. If human logic is worth anything at all we are simply driven to the conclusion that if my facts I have presented are true, man could never have done this."

A sampling of his discoveries was published, and is still being published today.

In the languages of both Hebrew and Greek which the Bible was written in, each letter has a numeric equivalent. These numbers have characteristics in the Bible that are unique and supernatural in origin. Let's look at just one fruit of his studies.

In the opening 11 verses of Matthew in the Greek did you know the...

Number of words

Number of letters

Number of consonants

Number of words beginning with a vowel

Number of words appearing more than once

Number of nouns

Number of names

Number of male names

Number of generations

… are all divisible by seven?

Seven is often used as the **number for God**. This begins with the Sabbath being the seventh day, God's day of rest, but continues throughout the scripture with an amazing incidence of the number.

For example Psalm 12:6 says… "The words of the Lord are pure words: as silver tried in a furnace of earth, purified seven times."

Throughout the book of Revelation there are also many patterns of seven.

To try to generate this sort of pattern that appears above would be inconceivable, yet this is just one example of the amazing numerical patterns that appear throughout the Bible. God has put His fingerprint on His word, and everywhere we look we see His guiding and inspiration behind the text.

In Conclusion

The Bible is God's Word.

We can see that the Bible through knowledge, prediction, unity, protection and preservation is shown to be not just any book. It is a message from the creator of the world to mankind that can be relied upon because it is divine in origin.

Both the Apostles Paul and Peter said the same thing too:

2 Timothy 3:16 *"All scripture is given by inspiration of God, and is profitable for doctrine, for reproof, for correction, for instruction in righteousness:"*

2 Peter 1:21 *"For the prophecy came not in old time by the will of man: but holy men of God spake as they were moved by the Holy Ghost."*

The Bible is indeed packed with ancient prophecies, miraculous foreknowledge and divine wisdom. The same God who spoke in the beginning, and created the earth by the word of his mouth, is the author of the Bible. His opinion is more important, more reliable and more powerful than any other opinion you will ever hear.

If you have been seeking the truth about all things, well done, you have found the ONE book that has it all!

I would encourage you to look further into this vast subject of God's word. At the back of the book is a selective Bibliography suggesting good books to aid with your further research into the Bible and its truths.

I cannot close this chapter without saying that once you begin to believe the Bible for what it is, it becomes a living book. When you come to know the author you find that He speaks today through His word, that it is a relevant and wonderful textbook for life, full of promises and truth that alone can lead you into a wonderful future.

To finish up, in this chapter we have seen...

- The Bible has knowledge not known to man at the time

- The Bible miraculously details Jesus' life in advance

- The Bible has been miraculously preserved and copied accurately

- The Bible is God's word

- The work of Ivan Panin

"When you have read the Bible, you will know it is the Word of God, because you will have found it the key to your own heart, your own happiness, and your own duty."

--Woodrow Wilson (1856-1924)
28th President of the United States

WORLD EMPIRES

DANIEL 7   DANIEL 2   REV 13

| Lion | Babylon
Head of
Gold | Lion |

| Bear | Medo Persia
Chest & Arms of
silver | Bear |

| Leopard | Greece
Belly of
Bronze | Leopard |

Rome
Legs of Iron

| Ten Headed
Beast | East   West | Ten Headed
Beast |

Rome 2
Feet of iron
& clay

CHAPTER 2

The World Empires

Worldempires were described beforehand by remarkable prophetic insight in the Bible.

In this chapter we will look at specific prophecies which give us details of empires that have already existed. These details will help us identify the last empire of human government, which is already forming EVEN AS WE SPEAK, but is not yet in its final phase.

The Statue of Man's Dominion

The remarkable details of major world empires were shown by God to King Nebuchadnezzar of Babylon in a dream, and were interpreted by the prophet Daniel.

Daniel had a close relationship with God and despite being deported from the royal courts in Jerusalem to Babylon his faith in God elevated him to a powerful position in the land.

While there were many wise men at the time who could suggest interpretations for the king's dream, the king was clever enough not to reveal the actual dream, so that he would know that the real interpreter had true, supernatural insight.

Daniel was the only one who could not only tell the King the dream, but also its interpretation. He went on to describe an image representing the world empires, beginning with Babylon, and ending with the Kingdom of God. He vividly outlined the major gentile world empires from the time of Nebuchadnezzar right up until the time of the Anti-Christ, the coming world leader who will head the last stage of the last empire.

This image has indeed so far been fulfilled in history with ASTONISHING accuracy, not bad considering the Book of Daniel was written way back in the sixth century BC.

Daniel 2:36-45 *"This was the dream, and now we will interpret it to the king. [37] Your Majesty, you are the king of kings. The God of heaven has given you dominion and power and might and glory; [38] in your hands He has placed all mankind and the beasts of the field and the birds in the sky. Wherever they live, He has made you ruler over them all. You are that head of gold.*

[39]After you, another kingdom will arise, inferior to yours. Next, a third kingdom, one of bronze, will rule over the whole earth. [40]Finally, there will be a fourth kingdom, strong as iron—for iron breaks and smashes everything—and as iron breaks things to pieces, so it will crush and break all the others.

[41]Just as you saw that the feet and toes were partly of baked clay and partly of iron, so this will be a divided kingdom; yet it will have some of the strength of iron in it, even as you saw iron mixed with clay. [42]As the toes were partly iron and partly clay, so this kingdom will be partly strong and partly brittle. [43]And just as you saw the iron mixed with baked clay, so the people will be a mixture and will not remain united, any more than iron mixes with clay.

[44]In the time of those kings, the God of heaven will set up a kingdom that will never be destroyed, nor will it be left to another people. It will crush all those kingdoms and bring them to an end, but it will itself endure forever. [45]This is the meaning of the vision of the rock cut out of a mountain, but not by human hands—a rock that broke the iron, the bronze, the clay, the silver and the gold to pieces."

Four Kingdoms

God showed to King Nebuchadnezzar in a dream, then interpreted by Daniel, and laid out throughout the book of Daniel for all willing to look, that four major empires were to arise before the last empire, during which the Lord Jesus Christ will also return to reign. This information is shown as a statue of a man made of different materials.

Let us look at this image...

The image is of a man, hence referring to human governments.

The materials decrease in value from the head down, gold, silver, bronze, iron, and iron and clay, but increase in strength, except for the iron and clay which does not mix well. This is where the well known saying "the statue has clay feet" comes from.

The first part is clear; it speaks of Babylon which is already in existence at the time. This is the head of gold and Daniel tells King Nebuchadnezzar just that.

Gold speaks of wealth, and Babylon was the wealthiest of the empires described and had huge military might.

Ruled by the mighty Nebuchadnezzar it stretched from North Africa to West Asia. The city of Babylon was awesome, and is said to have had double walls of 360 feet high and 87 feet wide running 15 miles square. Historians report chariot races of six abreast could be held on the tops of the wall. There were 250 watchtowers of 100 foot height on the second wall.

Details come from the writings of Heroditus the 'Father of History' and Xenophon, a student of Socrates. It was widely viewed as impervious to attack, completely impregnable, yet as we shall see shortly, that view proved wrong. When Cyrus surveyed Babylon's massive defences, he said: *"I am unable to see how any enemy can take walls of such strength and height by assault"* (Xenophon, VIII.V.7). However, with a stroke of pure genius he then devised a daring strategy that took the city as we shall see.

Each kingdom, we are told, was given dominion by God.

It is interesting to note the lesson in pride God gave to Nebuchadnezzar, he became as an animal for seven years (losing his mind) after taking the full credit for the might of his kingdom. While it was an awesome empire we all have to learn our frailty, and God warned Nebuchadnezzar what would happen should he succumb to pride. We read that as a result of his sin he was humbled, after which he then accepted that the God of heaven, Daniel's God, was the one true God above all others.

Daniel 4 is the King's account of what happened, which he had sent out throughout the known world. It is in a way one of the first tracts, and tells the world there is only one true God. It is heartening to know that God can reach even the most brutal of people.

Like Nebuchadnezzar we all need lessons in pride occasionally. We forget our frailty and the brevity of our lives at times and need to be reminded. Many proud and powerful kingdoms have passed into oblivion, but the word of God stands eternal, as will His coming kingdom.

It was at such a time of pride that Babylon was to finally fall, just as Daniel had predicted would happen. At that time the kingdom was in the hands of Belshazzar, son of King Nabonidus. While the Persians were invading the plains below the great might of the city itself must have made him feel very secure.

Like Titanic, the "unsinkable" ship, Babylon was thought safe. Belshazzar held a party, and took the vessels from the temple in Jerusalem when the Babylonians had ransacked Judah in 586BC, and used them for his party. He showed his contempt in doing this, taking items he knew the Jewish people held as holy, and using them in his wild party. Suddenly a hand appeared and wrote on the wall. Daniel was summoned to interpret the writing and it said...

"MENE, MENE, TEKEL, UPHARSIN"

The interpretation was...

Mene: God has numbered your kingdom and finished it;

Tekel: You have been weighed in the balance and found wanting;

Peres: Your kingdom has been divided and given to the Medes and Persians.

What happened next is documented in secular history too...

According to Herodotus the historian, that very night the Persians under King Cyrus took the city.

Herodotus writes of Cyrus' ingenious stratagem to enter the city:

". . . drawing off the river [Euphrates] by a canal into the lake, which was until now a marsh, he made the stream to sink till its former channel could be forded. When this happened, the Persians who were posted with this intent made their way into Babylon by the channel of the Euphrates, which had now sunk to about the height of the middle of a man's thigh."

The Euphrates flowed through the city of Babylon. Cyrus had it dammed higher up, and the armies of Persia were able to come in under the gates, the city fell without a battle and Belshazzar was slain the same night he had held the party and seen the writing on the wall.

The stele of Cyrus, currently in the British Museum, speaks of this very conquest.

This mighty city, seemingly impregnable, fell without a battle. It is said that some of the residents did not realize for three days what had happened. The might of impregnable Babylon was overcome just as Daniel said it would.

Furthermore, it must be noted that the Jews, including Daniel the prophet had been held captive in Babylon for 70 years. Jeremiah had predicted (25:8-14) that their captivity in Babylon would be 70 years.

This was fulfilled exactly.

It was 70 years from the time of their captivity in Babylon when Cyrus took Babylon and they were allowed to return to rebuild their own city. God had also revealed through Isaiah that after 70 years He would punish the king of Babylon which took place when King Cyrus took the city.

The head of gold, Babylon had passed.

A Second Empire arose

The kingdom that followed on from Babylon was the Medo Persian Empire of King Cyrus. This is represented by the arms and chest of silver. This was a vast empire, growing in strength but decreasing in value.

According to the Jewish writer Josephus, when King Cyrus read Isaiah 44b and 45, which was written over 150 years beforehand and clearly refers to Cyrus, not only by name, but with details, he was utterly convinced. The passage talks of the drying up of rivers, a reference to the Euphrates, and talks of Cyrus calling to build up Jerusalem again. Cyrus recognised this scripture was indeed speaking about him. As a result

King Cyrus showed leniency to the Jews, and encouraged them to go home and start the rebuilding of the temple.

Imagine how it would feel to know you had been written about by name long before you were born! Especially when the God of heaven wrote such good things about you!

God gives us glimpses of His glory through such things, which speak to us of His transcendence to even time itself. God knew about us also before we were born, and if we will only come to him, He has a wonderful plan for us even as He had for King Cyrus.

Look at these amazing verses from Isaiah:

44:27 *"That sayeth to the deep, be dry, and I will dry up thy rivers."*

45:1 *"Thus says the LORD to His anointed, To Cyrus, whose right hand I have held—to subdue nations before him…and have even called you by your name: I have named you, though you have not known Me I am the LORD, and there is no other;"*

The Persian Empire was not as wealthy as the Babylonian but exceeded its strength and size and continued for 200 years. This Kingdom was then conquered by Alexander the Great.

The chest and arms of silver, the second empire had passed.

The next world empire that arose was the Greek empire under Alexander the Great. This is represented by the thighs of brass.

It took Alexander only six years to conquer the mighty Medo-Persian Empire. By the time Alexander was thirty his empire stretched from the Mediterranean to Greece. He had amazing military prowess and conquered a vast area over a period of just twelve years, which stretched right into India. This empire again lessened in riches, but exceeded in might.

Alexander also had an encounter with God's foreknowledge… According to Josephus, on approaching Jerusalem to destroy it, he was met by a delegation led by the high priest. He was shown in the scripture references which he recognised as referring to him and spared the city as a result.

Awesome!

Here is what Josephus notes...

"When the book of Daniel was showed to him, wherein Daniel declared that one of the Greeks should destroy the empire of the Persians, he supposed that he was the person intended; and he was then glad." (Antiquities 11:8:5)

Alexander was so impressed by the Jews and their Bible that he allowed Jerusalem to remain semi-independent and for the Jews to practice their distinctive worship as long as they remained politically loyal to him.

It is stated that at 30 years old Alexander threw himself on his bed and said *"Why are there no more worlds to conquer?"*

Alexander died as a young man, 32 years old, and the empire was divided up to four generals; Cassandra, Ptolemy, Seleceus and Lysimicas.

Later chapters in the book of Daniel give a lot of these details containing amazing foreknowledge of this stage of the Greek empire. The critics have tried to tie the book to a later date as a way of explaining its accuracy, but the evidence for Daniel is strong. It is one of the most authenticated books of the Old Testament. As Daniel predicted, this empire also had its days numbered by the Lord.

The thighs of bronze had passed.

The Roman Empire

Next was the Roman Empire which conquered the Greek Empire, again less wealthy, but it was the mightiest, most vicious, and brutal empire. This was represented by the legs of iron.

Again it grew in might but receded in wealth. Covering much of North Africa, the Middle East, Asia and Europe it was indeed mighty.

Even today's government and laws have a lot of Roman influence. Unlike the other Empires, Rome wiped out former cultures and instituted its own police, justice and government. There were two legs, east and west. The western empire continued until 476AD, while the eastern leg continued until 1453AD. Rome surpassed the previous empires by its fearful might and longevity. All the other empires were clearly conquered but Rome broke up over time, rather than being conquered.

Pausing for a moment, to scan back over the vast sweep of world history, we can note that the legs of iron Daniel spoke of have passed...

Four key empires shown to the prophet Daniel have so far passed in history. What wonderful and accurate insight God blessed Daniel with, and how blessed we are to have God's word so we also can have insight from God concerning the world and its future.

The image Nebuchadnezzar saw finished with feet of iron and clay. This deserves VERY SPECIAL attention so we will deal with this, the last empire in the next chapter.

So far, we can see...

The bible is consistent in its predictions, and Daniel was further privileged to have another revelation confirming the dream of Nebuchadnezzar and his image of a man.

We read Daniel 7:1-8

"In the first year of Belshazzar king of Babylon, Daniel had a dream and visions of his head while on his bed. Then he wrote down the dream, telling the main facts.² Daniel spoke, saying, "I saw in my vision by night, and behold, the four winds of heaven were stirring up the Great Sea. ³ And four great beasts came up from the sea, each different from the other. ⁴ The first was like a lion, and had eagle's wings. I watched till its wings were plucked off; and it was lifted up from the earth and made to stand on two feet like a man, and a man's heart was given to it.
⁵And suddenly another beast, a second, like a bear. It was raised up on one side, and had three ribs in its mouth between its teeth. And they said thus to it: 'Arise, devour much flesh!'

⁶After this I looked, and there was another, like a leopard, which had on its back four wings of a bird. The beast also had four heads, and dominion was given to it.

⁷After this I saw in the night visions, and behold, a fourth beast, dreadful and terrible, exceedingly strong. It had huge iron teeth; it was devouring, breaking in pieces, and trampling the residue with its feet. It was different from all the beasts that were before it, and it had ten horns.⁸I was considering the horns, and there was another horn, a little one, coming up among them, before whom three of the first horns were plucked out by the roots. And there, in this horn, were eyes like the eyes of a man, and a mouth speaking pompous words."

This dream was received directly by Daniel himself.

He saw the same Kingdoms, but this time they were revealed as beasts.

The first was the lion.

This again spoke of Babylon. It had wings that were plucked, and it is true that after fast conquest Babylon ceased its advance and focused on building instead. The words about the heart of a man probably refer to the humbling of Nebuchadnezzar with seven years of insanity after having been the most powerful man on earth.

The second was the bear.

God showed the next Kingdom, Medo Persia as a bear. It was raised up on one side as Persia was the stronger side of the alliance. The three ribs probably refer to its three great conquests of Babylon, Egypt and Lydia. It was fearsome and vicious in its conquests, like a beast.

The third was the leopard.

This is a fast predator, and with wings, references the great speed with which Alexander conquered the known world. Alexander died young so the kingdom passed into the hands of four generals, Cassandra, Lysimicus, Seleuceus and Ptolemy. This explains the four heads Daniel speaks of.

The fourth beast portrayed Rome, a brutal empire. Unlike the others, instead of allowing some of the cultures and character of its conquests to remain it sought to wipe out all trace of them and impose its own character.

This time, to conclude, instead of ten toes we see ten horns.

This is significant because it portrays the re-emergence of the Roman Empire in a fashion. The little horn is also a clear reference to the coming world leader who will lead the final stage of world empires.

Just imagine that for a second, a world leader.

How many people have desired such a position throughout history, to RULE THE ENTIRE WORLD? Yet the Bible says that one man will eventually do just that, the Anti-Christ, which this very scripture highlights. More on him later though.

So we have a picture of four world empires; Babylon, Medo-Persia, Greece and Rome with one still to follow.

We see this same pattern in Revelation 13:1-2 *"Then I stood on the sand of the sea. And I saw a beast rising up out of the sea, having seven heads and ten horns, and on his horns ten crowns, and on his heads a blasphemous name. ²Now the beast which I saw was like a leopard, his feet were like the feet of a bear, and his mouth like the mouth of a lion."*

This is speaking of the last empire, and it seems to show it will have characteristics from the four empires - the leopard (Greece), the lion (Babylon), the bear (Medo-Persia) and of course the beast (Rome).

Again we have the number ten; ten toes (the image of Daniel 2), ten horns (the beast of Daniel 7) and ten horns and crowns (the beast of Rev 13)

Now...

Before we go on to look at this last world empire in the next chapter, let us remember God has His hand on history. He has allowed man free will, yet he knows all that is going to happen, and allows it for his own purposes. Ultimately these world empires will fade in the mists of time, and the time will come when Jesus Himself comes back to rule and reign. God showed this time to Daniel. He made it clear that these events would happen in the days of the last empire, so the next chapter is very important!

Daniel 7:13-14

"I was watching in the night visions,
And behold, One like the Son of Man,
Coming with the clouds of heaven!
He came to the Ancient of Days,
And they brought Him near before Him.
¹⁴Then to Him was given dominion and glory and a kingdom,
That all peoples, nations, and languages should serve Him.
His dominion is an everlasting dominion,

Which shall not pass away,
And His kingdom the one
Which shall not be destroyed."

The prophecies of world empires are wonderfully consistent. God has a plan from the creation of the world, to the days of a new heaven and a new earth. When earthly empires have faded and gone, God's eternal kingdom will remain.

So in this chapter we have seen...

- World Empires described in advance

- Nebuchadnezzar humbled

- King Cyrus spoken to by name in a text written 150 years before his time

- Alexander the Great recognizes himself in the Bible

"Indeed, it is an indisputable fact that all the complex and horrendous questions confronting us at home and worldwide have their answer in that single book [the Bible]."

--Ronald Reagan (1911-)
40th President of the United States

An Easy Guide To The End Times

CHAPTER 3

The Last Empire

Now we arrive at the Key Empire. The image from Daniel 2 finishes with the feet of iron and clay. This corresponds with the beast of Daniel 7 and Revelation 13.

These represent the last empire, and speak of a continuation of the Roman Empire. Bible prophesy is clear that the last world ruler, the Anti-Christ, and the last Empire will be linked to Rome. The Empire has weakness as iron which is strong, is mixed with clay which is weak. **Weak and strong nations will be unified.** This kingdom will be overcome when the Lord Jesus sets up His Government on earth. When we see this empire rising we know the coming of the Lord is near.

The fact that the last empire will be Rome is seen in...

Daniel 9:26 *"And the people of the prince who is to come shall destroy the city and the sanctuary."*

This was speaking of Jerusalem, and references when the Messiah (Jesus) was killed. It was fulfilled in history in 70AD when the Romans destroyed the city. "The people of the prince who is to come" was a reference to the world leader to come (the Anti-Christ). The people that destroyed the city were the Romans, so hence, the prince to come will be a Roman prince.

There have been a number of attempts to revive the Roman Empire. None of these were in the timing of God, who allows things in His time alone. It is sufficient (and comforting) to know that this timing fits with the world scene described in scripture, and one key component to note is seeing the nation of Israel re-established in their land in the Middle East. All is now fitting into place like a master jigsaw puzzle.

The Roman Empire is re-emerging today. Winston Churchill before he died said "We must build a United States of Europe"

This is happening as we speak.

We see today the reunification of much of Europe with the European Community, based on the Treaty of Rome, signed 25th March 1957. Based on its time of arising, geographical region and aims it is clear this is the start of the world's last empire.

Why?

Because in its final stage Rome will emerge as a ten nation confederacy that will gain power over the world as we have already seen from the scriptures in Daniel and Revelation.

While we are seeing only the start, yet it is clearly the beginning of the re-emergence of Rome. When one man becomes the head of the final form of this rising empire, and makes a seven year treaty with Israel we will know the Anti-Christ has come, and we are living in the last empire of all.

I believe the European Union could very well be that empire.

Here is why...

Some of the features of the EU that should cause us concern are as follows :

- The aim to federalise, lessening each countrie's individual power and creating an integrated union and gradually transferring powers from individual governments.

- The EU Constitution has many worrying features, such as new laws which threaten our liberty and freedom of speech. This is marked by political correctness.

- Moves towards a common currency (the Euro).

- The emergence of a European army, independent of NATO.

- The use of large and powerful computers in Europe to control every individual in the EU.

- The movement to globalisation.

These aims may not all be realised, but are setting the scene for the rise of the worst despot ever known. This last empire is going to have great dominion. In the chapter on the world leader later, we shall see how the world is being prepared for such a global leader. The world is also being prepared for a global government which will be based in Europe.

There are many conspiracy theories concerning the rise of despotic world government, and these are not all without some solid evidence.

There is now little doubt that many prominent people have been planning a New World Order behind the scenes for a long time and these plans are fast advancing.

The "New World Order" (NWO) once a term used rarely, has become much more blatant these days. This new order expressly strives to bring in a new Global government that seeks to control every single human on earth.

George Bush senior and junior, Mikhail Gorbachof, Tony Blair, Gordon Brown, Henry Kissinger and many other world figures have all spoken of the need for this new order. The background of the NWO is laced in mystery, occultism and secret organisations, as we shall see in our studies.

Benjamin Disraeli said...

"So you see the world is ruled by very different personages than what is imagined by those who are not themselves behind the scenes."

Hence many shadowy figures are hard at work behind the scenes to produce a world government. There are countless books on these issues, but it is clear that plans for a world government are well advanced (though most know nothing of them at all) and that the re-emergence of the Roman Empire in the guise of the European Union is a key factor.

While many secret and mystical organisations are involved such as The Illuminati, the Freemasons, the Bilderbergers, The Club of Rome, and

The Council on Foreign Relations, they themselves are just puppets of Satan (or Lucifer) who is behind these plans and cleverly orchestrating them in the spiritual realm.

Satan was behind the manoeuvrings that lead to Jesus being crucified, and believed he had won the battle, not realising the crucifixion was part of God's plan all along. What looked like a tragedy turned into the great victory when Jesus rose from the dead. Likewise God is allowing evil to come to a head in these last days but will intervene at the last moment. It is God alone who has the timing of the last empire in His hands, and it will happen only when he deems it right to allow.

One of the strange evidences of hidden forces at work is the seal on the American one dollar bill. Full of esoteric and occult symbolism there has never been a good reason given for the placing of this seal.

The seal declares:

Annuit Septis: announcing the birth of.

Novus Ordo Seclorium: a new secular world order.

Why would the dollar bill have this strange seal, and announcement?

There is a pyramid, an occult symbol itself; on the elevated capstone of the pyramid is the symbol, the eye of Lucifer or the eye of Horus. The innuendo is that at the top of the pyramid, the top of the world powers is none other than Satan. Whoever therefore put this in place is declaring the new world order intends to enthrone Lucifer as head.

There are those with influence in the Government of America deeply involved in plans for the new world order. Many American Presidents have been in the mystical and shadowy world of freemasonry, many have been high level masons. This is clearly evidenced in history, and may well explain the Masonic symbols placed all over Washington Dc, not least the square and compass built into the street patterns as seen from the air.

One Masonic writer, Manly Hall, declares that some of America's founders were funded by secret societies with the clear purpose of founding this Godless new world order. Freemasonry is an organization full of darkness.

The true God is a God of openness and truth, whilst masonry is secretive. Its symbolism alone is enough to warn of its mystical and demonic roots. Its beliefs are now well published by former members and are clearly incompatible with biblical Christianity. Masonry certainly has involvements with plans for world government.

Much has been written about the plethora of mystical symbols on the dollar bill. For our part it points to the fact there are clearly forces at work to bring about a centralised world government.

This may all seem very bizarre, yet there are many influential people declaring their desire for, and clearly involved in this move towards world government.

Let's look at some of these below...

David Rockefeller responded to charges that he wanted a global government ruled by an 'elite' that he was "guilty and proud of it."

George Bush:

"What is at stake is more than one small country, it is a big idea–a new world order... to achieve the universal aspirations of mankind... based on shared principles and the rule of law... The illumination of a thousand points of light... The winds of change are with us now?"

Henry Kissinger:

"[The New World Order] cannot happen without U.S. participation, as we are the most significant single component. Yes, there will be a New World Order, and it will force the United States to change its perceptions."

David Rockefeller in an address to a Trilateral Commission meeting in June of 1991:

"We are grateful to the Washington Post, the New York Times, Time magazine and other great publications whose directors have attended our meetings and respected the promises of discretion for almost forty years. It would have been impossible for us to develop our plan for the world if we had been subject to the bright lights of publicity during those years. But, the world is now more sophisticated and prepared to march towards a world-government. The supranational sovereignty of an intellectual elite and world bankers is surely preferable to the National auto determination practised in past centuries."

Mikhail Gorbachev:

"Further global progress is now possible only through a quest for universal consensus in the movement towards a new world order."

January 2nd, 2004 - CNN

"Vatican City, Pope John Paul II rang in the New Year on Thursday with a renewed call for peace in the Middle East and Africa and the creation of a new world order based on respect for the dignity of man and equality among nations." (World News 24.com Jan 4th 2004)

"Today the impulse towards interdependence is immeasurably greater. We are witnessing the beginnings of a new doctrine of international community."

Tony Blair (Speaking April 22nd 1999 at the Chicago Economic Club)

Gordon Brown today called for a "new global order" to deal with the economic crisis as he warned against the protectionist policies of the 1930s. (The Guardian 26th Jan 2009)

"Recession is the birth pangs of a new global order" said Gordon Brown (Daily Mail 27th January 2009)

He also addressed the Yorkshire Business Conference in 2009 and said *"Globalisation of Business means nation's state is on the way out."*

"Senior Eurocrats are secretly plotting to create a super-powerful EU president to realise their dream of abolishing Britain, we can reveal. Opponents fear the plan could create a modern-day equivalent of the European emperor envisaged by Napoleon Bonaparte or a return to the Holy Roman Empire of Charlemagne that dominated Europe in the Dark Ages." (Daily Express Friday May 4th 2012.)

There is little doubt that behind the scenes much more is happening than we know about. Certainly the current financial crisis and European problems are being used to bring in much greater regulation, and at present the financial crisis looks like being used to propel Europe into greater union.

Some of the preparations we see for this coming new order are easy to spot...

- **Interdependence:**

  Nations are becoming more and more dependent, even national services such as water are being sold to foreign investors. Nations are becoming reliant on other nations to survive. The aim is that no country will be permitted to survive on its own, because all will need one another.

- **Globalisation:**

  Already huge companies are growing still larger and taking over the lesser, forming vast multi-national corporations. The communications network is turning the world into the global village. The world has changed vastly in 50 years and that advance continues. These companies have great power to control through controlling resources at source.

Lord Healey said... *"To say we were striving for a one-world government is exaggerated, but not wholly unfair. Those of us in Bilderberg felt we couldn't go on forever fighting one another for nothing and killing people and rendering millions homeless. So we felt that a single community throughout the world would be a good thing."* (The Guardian 14th May 2009)

- There is much talk of globalising the monetary systems, and forming a common currency.

- There are worldwide trends towards saving the planet. Despite the very questionable science on which Global warming has been based, its many critics say it is being used as an international agenda to join nations together in a fight against a common enemy. While we should do all we can to protect the planet God has given us it is very obvious there are political manoeuvrings behind these current agendas.

Key Groups involved in World Government plans include...

- The Bilderbergers

- Council of Foreign Relations

- The Trilateral Commission

- The Freemasons

- And many more...

Early in history we read that Nimrod built a city, and began building a tower called the tower of Babel. The name Nimrod means "I will rebel".

In building a city he was going against God's command to spread out and repopulate the earth. The tower of Babel, an enormous religious tower was a direct act against God instituting false worship. God came down and destroyed what happened at Babel and confused their languages, thus causing a scattering of the peoples. Many prominent philologists recognize that all the languages indeed came from one original language.

Given God's attitude to the tower of Babel you would think that no-one would try again. However, in a sense both the European Union and the world government are working towards a new tower of Babel. It is no coincidence that the following poster was used for the European Union.

The European parliament building was actually based on this painting of the tower of Babel painted by Peter Brueghel in the 1500's, and used in this EU poster as seen below.

The Parliament Building

How foolish can man be?

A reporter questioning "Why the Tower of Babel" as a design concept was answered in an astounding way by an EU official. He said, *"What they failed to complete 3000 years ago – we in Europe will finish now!"*

Amazingly Europe has also used symbolism related to the book of Revelation to portray its own vision of the future.

Quite stunning because...

In Revelation we see a woman riding the beast that represents the last

An Easy Guide To The End Times

world empire. This same picture is used on several European coins and is a statue outside the parliament.

This should come as no surprise to careful students of scripture and the times we live in today.

So to conclude this chapter...

We are *already* living in the days of the rise of the last world empire. When it fully arises, one man will become the head, a seven year peace treaty will be agreed in the Middle East, and nations will conspire against Israel. When you see these things line up, it is at that point you will know that EVEN THE LAST SEVEN YEARS themselves of the very final age has finally come!

WARNING: It is not very far away at all.

In this chapter we have learned...

- Last world Empire begins to arise

- Plans for world government

- New Tower of Babel

"It is impossible to mentally or socially enslave a Bible-reading people."

--Horace Greeley (1811-1872)
Publisher and Journalist

An Easy Guide To The End Times

FOUR HORSEMEN OF THE APOCOLYPSE

WHITE HORSE	RED HORSE	BLACK HORSE	PALE HORSE
False Christ False Peace	War	Hyper-inflation Famine Poverty	Death of Multitudes

CHAPTER 4

The Final World Leader

As we have established the last world empire will be a re-emergence of the Roman Empire and will arise in the same region. This will be headed up by a man spoken of and described thousands of years ago. He will come in times of crisis offering the world answers to seemingly intractable problems, and will quickly rise to power as he gains adulation by the masses as he "miraculously" applies solutions that appear to work initially. The world at this stage will look for a great leader to rescue them, and this man, seemingly a saviour offering the world peace and prosperity will fit the bill perfectly. However he will soon be revealed as a devil, despot, and a truly corrupt, evil man.

Many believe this man is alive today!

The Bible, both Old and New Testaments, speaks of this man, who will be the culmination of the reign of human government, and will epitomise the pride of man. In the Bible 6 is the number of man, this man's number will be 666, and he will be a man who seeks to take God's place. He will fall just like others before him though, who have been deceived by the pride of their own hearts.

While it is hard to consider that the world will adulate such a man, history shows men of great charisma can gain great power. Hitler was just one example. Those who attended the Nuremberg rallies say the atmosphere was so electric it was hard not to be swept up by it. Hitler seized power at a time of great difficulty for the German people because he seemed to have plausible answers and strong arguments to back up his solutions. Many leaders throughout history have gained great adulation, and have known how to manipulate and brainwash the masses in order to execute their own agendas whether good or evil.

History will most certainly repeat itself.

"The only thing we learn from history is that we learn nothing from history." So said Friedrich Hegel rather tellingly.

Some of the names of this coming leader are:

- The Seed of Satan (Genesis 3:15)

- The Little Horn (Daniel 7:8)

- The King of Fierce Countenance (Daniel 8:23)

- The Prince That Shall Come (Daniel 9:26)

- The Desolator (Daniel 9:27)

- The Wilful King (Daniel 11:36)

- The Man of Sin (2 Thessalonians 2:3)

- The Son of Perdition (2 Thessalonians 2:3)

- The Lawless One (2 Thessalonians 2:8)

- The Antichrist (1 John 2:22)

- The Beast (Revelation 11:7)

- The Assyrian (Isaiah 14)

- The First Horseman (Revelation 5)

- The Wicked One (2 Thessalonians 2:3-8)

- The Idol Shepherd (Zechariah 11:17)

- The Vile Person (Daniel 11)

- The One Who Comes In His Own Name (John 5:43)

- The son of Perdition (2 Thessalonians 2-3)

He is referred to so many times and in so many parts of scripture; this suggests how important it is to know who he is. This man will become the most dangerous man the world has ever encountered because the Devil will actually enter him and live through him, yet he will appear to be the opposite, sweetness, light and proponent of all that is good.

He will come as a loving saviour with all the answers, yet Paul the apostle warned us that the devil often comes as an angel of light. His true nature will soon be exposed once he gains power.

Methods of Accession

To gain power he will not at first use military might, instead he will accede through deceit and the promise of world peace and times of safety.

I Thessalonians 5 *"But concerning the times and the seasons, brethren, you have no need that I should write to you.²For you yourselves know perfectly that the day of the Lord so comes as a thief in the night³For when they say, "Peace and safety!" then sudden destruction comes upon them, as labour pains upon a pregnant woman. And they shall not escape."*

Peace and safety will be the words on the lips of this man who makes great promises. But be forewarned, Jesus, who is referred to in the Bible as the TRUE Prince of Peace (Isaiah 9:6) warns that there will be wars and rumours of wars right up until the end of the age. Therefore we know that anyone who comes with talk of world peace is an impostor.

In Daniel 8:25 we read...

*"Through his cunning He shall cause deceit to prosper under his rule;
And he shall exalt himself in his heart.
He shall destroy many in their prosperity.
He shall even rise against the Prince of princes;
But he shall be broken without human means."*

Deceit and cunning will mark him therefore.

God is NOT deceived by him of course...

The book of Revelation speaks of a scroll, that when opened starts the events of the end of the age. It is important to realise therefore that it is

God who is in control, and is allowing good and evil to take their course, ultimately so that He alone will separate good and evil forever.

Revelation 5:1-3 *"And I saw in the right hand of Him who sat on the throne a scroll written inside and on the back, sealed with seven seals.² Then I saw a strong angel proclaiming with a loud voice, "Who is worthy to open the scroll and to loose its seals?" ³And no one in heaven or on the earth or under the earth was able to open the scroll, or to look at it."*

This scroll is significant, because its opening is sanctioned by God himself, and releases the events of the rise of the Anti-Christ, the world leader.

This scroll is written on the back and front. This was unusual, and was usually the mark of a title deed in ancient times. It seems this could be the title deed for planet earth, which for legal reasons of redemption could only be opened by Jesus Christ, the original owner.

These seals as they are broken are all part of the process that will bring the earth back to its original ownership. Adam lost his tenancy of Earth to Lucifer, the devil in the Garden of Eden, and so Lucifer is presently god of this world as the Apostle Paul states (2 Corinthians 4:4). God is going to take back the tenancy and present it to the Lord Jesus who will rule and reign. What a day that will be!

Revelation 11:15 *"The kingdoms of this world have become the kingdoms of our God and of His Christ and He shall reign forever and ever."*

As the seals of the scroll are opened the four horsemen go forth...

Four Horsemen of the Apocalypse

First Horse; White, Gives False Peace

Revelation 5:1-2 *"Now I saw when the Lamb opened one of the seals; and I heard one of the four living creatures saying with a voice like thunder, "Come and see." ²And I looked, and behold, a white horse. He who sat on it had a bow; and a crown was given to him, and he went out conquering and to conquer."*

The first horse that comes is the white horse. This is a war horse and speaks of conquest. This is with peace; he carries a bow but no arrow. His initial conquest will be by peace and subtlety. This bow is also a symbol of covenant, just as God gave Noah the rainbow as a sign of His promise. This man will make covenants, but will break them.

The rider of the white horse is certainly not the Lord Jesus Christ, he appears later in Revelation, and is easily identified. No, what we are being shown here by the scripture is a false Christ, an impostor.

Part of this imposter's promises of peace will lead to a treaty in the Middle East. This has already been worked at for many years, yet currently it seems a near impossibility to even think a peace could exist between Israel and its neighbours. God also told us that Jerusalem would be the centre of trouble.

Zechariah 12:3 *"And it shall happen in that day that I will make Jerusalem a heavy stone for all peoples; all who heave away at it will surely be cut in pieces, though all nations of the earth are gathered against it."*

Daniel 9:27 *"Then he shall confirm a covenant with many for one week; But in the middle of the week He shall bring an end to sacrifice and offering."*

From the above verses we see this "Man of Peace" appearing to solve the age old enmity and bring peace between Israel and its enemies. He will agree to allow sacrifices and offering to continue in a newly established Temple, but will then break his promise after three and a half years.

This "week" referred to above in Daniel 9 specifies a Biblical term meaning "a week" of years, which is a seven year period. This seven year period is referred to elsewhere.

This man, also known as the Anti-Cchrist will deceive; his methods will be cunning, but ruthless as the Apostle Paul explains...

2 Thessalonians 2:9-10 *"The coming of the lawless one is according to the working of Satan, with all power, signs, and lying wonders, and with all unrighteous deception among those who perish, because they did not receive the love of the truth, that they might be saved."*

His methods will major in deception. He will be endued with Satanic power. Just as God the Father sent his son, and then the Holy Spirit, so this man will be, in essence the son of Satan and will work with another man who is known as the false Prophet (Rev 13:1-13).

Therefore we can see that the scripture warns that even as a counterfeit of God's Holy Trinity, there will be a satanic trinity which includes the Devil, the Anti-Christ and the False Prophet.

In a similar way that Jesus died and rose again this man too will suffer a mortal wound, but somehow live. Again this represents a counterfeiting of the resurrection of the Lord Jesus.

Revelation 13:3 *"And I saw one of his heads as if it had been mortally wounded, and his deadly wound was healed. And all the world marvelled and followed the beast."*

In Revelation 13:2 we read... *"The dragon gave him his power, his throne and great authority."*

This man, the Anti-Christ, will display supernatural signs and also lying signs. He may well use technology to produce some of these. Nations will be amazed at his power and will be taken in. The white horse speaks of the rise of this man.

Second Horse; Red War

Despite the Anti-Christ's promises of peace, war will soon be on its way, and he will destroy anyone who stands in his way. Part of his war will involve the invasion of Israel. As we have already seen 1 Thessalonians 5 warns when peace and safety is offered sudden destruction will come.

Suddenly all of the promises of peace and prosperity will be revealed as no more than a power play. The Anti-Christ's rise to power will be through cunning and false promises. Jesus warned us that one of the signs of the end would be wars and rumours of wars (Matthew 24:6).

Third Horse; Black Hyper Inflation

The Bible warns us of a time when money will be worthless.

James 1:1-3 *"Come now, you rich, weep and howl for your miseries that are coming upon you! ²Your riches are corrupted, and your garments are moth-eaten ³Your gold and silver are corroded, and their corrosion will be a witness against you and will eat your flesh like fire. You have heaped up treasure in the last days."*

Not only will there be massive inflation, but this man intends to use money to control and enslave. The Proverbs remind us that the borrower is servant to the lender. Today many people are in trouble through debt.

Now is the time to use wisdom and do our utmost to get free, pay debt down, and be much wiser with our spending. The Bible includes a special warning for the rich. Money is a useful tool, but it cannot bring happiness. We only have to read the daily papers to learn how many of the rich and famous have huge problems and difficulties.

The wise man will put his faith in eternal things and store up treasure in heaven by putting God first in their lives, rather than depending on the rewards of the world system of money, which will soon revealed as completely worthless when the Anti-Christ seizes control.

There will come a time when this leader will also introduce a mark that will be essential to buy or sell. There will be famine and scarcity.

Thankfully God has forewarned us in the Book of Revelation so we need not fear or be sucked into accepting this mark which all humans will be required to be branded by on pain of death.

Revelation 13:16-18 *"He causes all, both small and great, rich and poor, free and slave, to receive a mark on their right hand or on their foreheads, [17] and that no one may buy or sell except one who has the mark or the name of the beast, or the number of his name. [18] Here is wisdom. Let him who has understanding calculate the number of the beast, for it is the number of a man: His number is 666."*

This mark will signify allegiance to this leader. We are warned that all who take it will suffer eternal punishment.

Whilst this mark is a mark of ownership, true Christians already have a mark concerning their ownership, in Ephesians 1:13... *"In whom ye also trusted, after that ye heard the word of truth, the gospel of your salvation: in whom also after that ye believed, ye were sealed with that Holy Spirit of promise."*

We are told that having believed we are sealed with the Holy Spirit. At the point when the mark of the beast becomes compulsory Christians will have been taken away. More on this later.

Those who have become Christians after Jesus returned to take his own away may well have to make a choice between martyrdom and receiving the mark.

Science Agrees With The Book of Revelation!

The Greek word for mark - charagma - speaks of being pricked or marked. It could speak of a visible mark, or an implanted microchip. In Strong's concordance it is translated as an etching, a mark providing undeniable identification.

Many believe current technology which implants credit card information under the skin and is powered by lithium will be used. Pets are currently micro-chipped in such a way to identify them and protect them from theft, and even some famous people have allegedly already been micro-chipped. As far back as 1992 the Sunday Star Computing Magazine advertised...

"A new concept implants a chip in your body for access to a world of benefits."

There are certainly plans afoot to do away with cash and implement a credit system already as we will see shortly. This will do away with tax fraud, and have many logical benefits, but could easily be used in the wrong way.

Strangely in Australia a number of cartoons appeared in newspapers showing people bearing marks on their body connected with identification and credit, one with a mark on the forehead, showing it being scanned at the supermarket checkout. Some of these cartoons showed the number 666.

A friend of ours at the time investigated the source and claimed he found evidence of the funding from the Australian government. It certainly raises questions as to why these cartoons should appear, as the subject is far from humorous.

The Daily Telegraph featured an article on 11th January 2010...

"Is a cashless society on the cards? Steve Perry, executive vice president of Visa Europe, says cash is expensive, a cost on society, and should be replaced by a cashless society."

The article goes on to detail the problems with cash.

In May 2012 the European branch of the ATM Association met in London. Here are some excerpts from their comments on the cashless society...

"Thus interesting to see the first plenary presentation by Ramiro Sánchez-Crespo, from la Caixa (Spain) entitled "ATM in a Contactless World."

During this presentation he told of a three stage project by this Barcelona-based bank (which is, by the way, the second or third largest domestic player).

The first trial took place in the small coastal town of Sitges. Interestingly, this town appears several times in the history of Spanish computing, more than likely because of its demographics rather than chance. Here about 1,000 pre-prepared mobiles were distributed for a mobile-only payment trial.

Feedback led to the introduction of mobile and contactless cards, this time in the Balearic Islands. A third larger trial is currently underway across the city of Barcelona. This involves mobile, contactless cards and the deployment of a new, contact-less ATM model.

The Daily Mirror in August 1993 got it wrong by declaring cash would be dead by the year 2000. However, the technology they wrote of is now readily available.

Recent adverts have declared openly "cash will soon be dead"- Billboard adverts for Barclays bank last year...

BARCLAYS
RESEARCH FINDS BRITS DON'T
LIKE BULGING POCKETS
AND CASH MAY SOON BE DEAD

Back in May 17th 1992 the Sunday Star Computing Magazine showed a bare chested man with a computer chip on him, and declared "Power under your skin - New Concept Implants Chip in Your Body For Access to a World of Benefits."

On August 4th 2011 creditcards.com published an article entitled "Britons Anticipate Cash Free Future." It went on to say many believe that cash will die out completely. They detailed a Barclaycard survey about awareness of contactless technology, and they found the following...

- 44% recognises the contactless logo at the point of sale, up from 28% a year ago.

- 62% were aware of what contactless cards can do, up from 45% a year ago.

"Although we are far from becoming a 'cashless society', it's clear from our research that cash is no longer king," says Dan Wass, head of current accounts and contactless at Barclays. *"Consumers are increasingly less willing to carry*

large amounts of change around with them and many believe that coins will become obsolete in the future. It is clear that shoppers are now looking for alternative methods of payment — such as contactless — which will allow them to avoid spending time fumbling for change in a queue and will take up less space in their wallet."

There is definitely a move away from cash. Plastic cards will soon be obsolete, with microchips replacing them. Contactless cards are already available. Reliance on cards and technology means all a person's spending habits and whereabouts can also be very easily traced. These plastic cards have problems, they can be lost, stolen or counterfeited. Billions of pounds per year are currently lost through fraud. To put a chip in the body would solve many of these problems. This is all part of Anti-Christ plan to control and subjugate the entire global populace.

There have been many mentions of a one-world currency.

For example, The Institute of International Finance, a group that represents 420 of the world's largest banks and finance houses, has issued yet another call for a one-world global currency, as Jerome Corsi's Red Alert reports...

"A core group of the world's leading economies need to come together and hammer out an understanding," Charles Dallara, the Institute of International Finance's managing director, told the Financial Times. An IIF policy letter authored by Dallara and dated October 4th 2011 made clear that global currency coordination was needed, in the group's view, to prevent a *"looming currency war".*

It is certain, whatever form this mark takes it will signify allegiance to the Anti-Christ, and without it a person will not be able to buy or sell.

WARNING: The Bible specifically states that if anyone takes this mark they will NOT be able to gain entrance to heaven (**Revelation 14:9-10**) so DO NOT take it!

The aim of all these moves is to enable the Anti-Christ and his world government to gain total control and usher in the complete enslavement of the entire world's population.

Forth Horse: Pale Death and Hades

Towards the end of this world leader's reign he will set up his own image in the Jewish temple, which will be restored at this time. This is the final act of defiance towards God. Catastrophic devastation will ensue, not only due to the Anti-Christ's reign and policies, but also because the judgement of God by this stage will start to be revealed against mankind.

Why?

Well, God has done all he can to let people know what will happen, and to give them a chance to repent and receive His forgiveness, but for those who will not there must be justice, because God is holy. Everything in us tells us when a crime is committed there must be justice, and God, in His justice has to judge an unbelieving and rebellious world, giving a last chance for people to repent. The last seven years of the age will be the worst time in history even surpassing the events of the holocaust.

Matthew 24:21 *"For then shall be great tribulation, such as was not since the beginning of the world to this time, no, nor ever shall be."*

Considering the times the world has been through this is a mind blowing statement, and is a time when we certainly do not want to be here.

Judgement came during the time of Noah. The people then were warned many times it was coming, yet they wilfully ignored those warnings. We are told that Noah preached righteousness. There was also a man named Enoch who was a prophet. He was the first one that prophesied the second coming of Jesus at the end of the age (Jude 1:14). He had a son called Methuselah, which means "when he dies it shall come". There is little doubt this was a warning of the coming flood which Enoch would have warned of. In the exact year Methuselah died we see that the flood did come. For all who entered the ark though, there was life.

This is true of our day. Jesus Christ is our Ark. If we will trust in Him and His sacrifice for our safety we will also be lifted out before judgement comes.

How can we recognise the Anti-Christ?

The chief characteristic of this leader will be his boasting and arrogance. He will think himself invincible and shamelessly promote himself.

Energised by satanic power he will totally oppose Biblical Christians, and ultimately will set himself up as god, demanding worship, and force all his followers to accept a mark of allegiance.

We read in Daniel 7:11... *"I watched then because of the sound of the pompous words which the horn was speaking."*

Revelation 13:5 *"And he was given a mouth speaking great things and blasphemies."*

2 Thessalonians 2:3-4 *"...the son of perdition who opposes and exalts himself above all that is called God or that is worshipped, so that he sits as God in the temple of God, showing himself that he is God."*

Daniel 11:36 *"Then the king shall do according to his own will: he shall exalt and magnify himself above every god, shall speak blasphemies against the God of Gods."*

This man will be boastful, and deluded. His aim will be total control, he will demand worship from the people of every nation.

True Christians need not worry however, because they will have been taken up in the rapture of the Church (Luke 21:36) and will not remain on earth during this terrible reign of the Anti-Christ.

Those who become believers after this event will face a difficult time though, and many will be martyred rather than swear allegiance to the Antichrist.

So concerning the Anti-Christ...

- He can be recognised

- He will head a new Roman empire

- He will initiate a seven year Middle East treaty

- He will be very boastful

- He will promise peace and prosperity

- He will hate Christians

- He will declare himself god

- He will bring in a mark of allegiance

He will set up his own image in the Jewish temple. He has many names and faces for every occasion, seeming to have all the answers. He will be a man who will seem to be the answer to the problems of the world, to the Jews he will be Messiah, to the Buddhists the fifth reincarnation of Buddha, to the Christians he will claim to be Christ. In essence he will claim to be the expected Messiah for all faiths.

He will quickly gain power, and be adulated, but the world's joy will quickly turn to horror as he demands worship, and heralds the start of the dramatically catastrophic events of the book of Revelation.

Some are openly calling for this man to come even now...

Paul Henri-Spaak (1899-1972), the former Prime Minister of Belgium, the first Chairman of the General Assembly of the United Nations (1945), and one of the key founders of the movement toward European unity said...

"We do not want another committee. We have too many already. What we want is a man of sufficient stature to hold the allegiance of all people, and to lift us out of the economic morass in which we are sinking. Send us such a man and, be he God or the devil, we will receive him."

"The Council on Foreign Relations (CFR) is the American Branch of a society which originated in England (and) believes national boundaries should be obliterated and one-world rule established." - Professor of History Carroll Quigley, Georgetown University, in his book "Tragedy and Hope".

Dr. Henry Kissinger at the Bilderberger Conference, Evians, France, 1991...

"Today, America would be outraged if U.N. troops entered Los Angeles to restore order. Tomorrow they will be grateful! This is especially true if they were told that there were an outside threat from beyond, whether real or promulgated, that threatened our very existence. It is then that all peoples

of the world will plead to deliver them from this evil. The one thing every man fears is the unknown. When presented with this scenario, individual rights will be willingly relinquished for the guarantee of their well-being granted to them by the World Government."

The proponents of world government are clear that they want a one world leader. The Bible tells us such a world leader will come, and details his life and career, and warns us to have nothing to do with him because of the terrible consequences.

However...

There is a way of escape, God makes sure there always is, and His Way is through a man too... Jesus Christ, the Son of God Himself.

You see...

Jesus Christ made a way for all who will follow him to escape the things that will come on earth, and the terror of the last seven years of world history. If we have a relationship with him we will be taken out of the picture before the worst time in history.

Just as God took Noah away before the flood and rescued Lot out of Sodom before the fire, if we put our faith in God, and his **redemptive work on the cross** we will likewise be taken out before these things take place. This redemptive work refers to the way something is paid for. It is a word still used for mortgages, when the price is paid the mortgage is redeemed.

A slave when paid for and set free was said to have been redeemed.

Likewise if we, who have all been tainted by sins power, trust in the price that Jesus paid by dying on the cross can also experience redemption. It is only through being redeemed that we have any way of knowing God, or coming into the presence of Him who is holy. The good news is that as we trust in Christ we will be rescued from the terrible judgement that is coming.

Luke 21:36 *"Watch ye therefore, and pray always, that ye may be accounted worthy to escape all these things that shall come to pass and to stand before the Son of Man."*

To sum up, in this chapter we have learned…

- Charismatic World Leader to arise

- Mark of the beast now possible

- God preparing to remove His people

- Four Horsemen of the Apocalypse to be released

"No one ever said at the end of his days; 'I have read my BIBLE too much, I have thought of God too much, I have prayed too much, I have been too careful with my soul'"

J.C. Ryle

CHAPTER FIVE
Israel: A Sign to the Nations

Israel and the Jews are very significant in God's eternal plan. God made unconditional promises to them thousands of years ago, some of which are yet to be fulfilled. They are key in their role in end time prophecy, and are also a major sign to all that God always keeps his word. Their very existence as a nation powerfully underlines that this age is close to its end. This is because when you look at the fulfilment of prophecy concerning Israel, you will see stunning evidence that Gods word will ALWAYS be fulfilled despite at times what seems overwhelming odds against the likelihood of that happening.

Let's look at some of the fulfilled predictions to kick us off...

Jesus, speaking beforehand, referred to the time of the destruction of Jerusalem, its temple and the dispersal of the Jews. He also referred to Daniel's words about events yet to happen in Jerusalem.

Let's look at the first three events he spoke of...

Luke 19:43-44 *"For days will come upon you when your enemies will build an embankment around you, surround you and close you in on every side, ⁴⁴ and level you, and your children within you, to the ground; and they will not leave in you one stone upon another, because you did not know the time of your visitation."*

Daniel 9:26b *"The people of the prince who is to come shall destroy the city and the sanctuary."*

Jesus in his Olivet discourse in Matthew 24 refers to the coming destruction of the temple...

Matthew 24:1-2 *"Then Jesus went out and departed from the temple, and His disciples came up to him the buildings of the temple. And Jesus said to them, "Do you not see all these things? Assuredly I say unto you, not one stone shall be left here upon another, that shall not be thrown down."*

Luke 19:24 *"And they will fall by the edge of the sword, and be led away captive into all nations. And Jerusalem will be trampled by Gentiles until the times of the Gentiles are fulfilled."*

The predictions in these verses are vividly clear and indeed have all been fulfilled! How definite God can be! Who would dare to make such clear statements at the risk of being discredited?

Daniel's words came hundreds of years before. His statements placed these events after the Messiah (Jesus) had arrived and was to be executed. Jesus confirmed Daniel's words and even goes on to give more detail. What is beyond dispute is that both Daniel's words and the words of Jesus are from well before the events took place, and are EXTREMELY clear in their meaning.

Fulfilment...

It was in 66AD that Vespasian and the Roman armies came against Jerusalem. On hearing he was to be the next emperor Vespasian returned to Rome and removed the siege from Jerusalem. This gave time for those who understood what Jesus had told them when He said to flee Jerusalem in Luke 21:20-21...

"And when ye shall see Jerusalem compassed with armies, then know that the desolation thereof is nigh. Then let them which are in Judaea flee to the mountains; and let them which are in the midst of it depart out; and let not them that are in the countries enter thereinto."

They fled to a place called Pella which is in modern day Jordan, about two and a half miles east of the Jordan river. Josephus the Historian wrote of this event. Eusebius, 4th century Christian historian also recorded these events.

As a result Hebrew Christians escaped the terrible carnage that was to come because they believed and followed Jesus' words. Four years later in 70AD Titus returned with the Roman armies and Jerusalem was destroyed exactly as was foretold. Embankments were indeed raised around the city. Josephus records that over one million died and 97,000 were sold into slavery. Other reports give even larger figures.

Jesus' words about Herod's temple, which was a magnificent enormous building, were fulfilled in a very literal way. During the invasion the temple was set alight, and the gold from the ornaments melted and ran between the stones. For some time people moved stones trying to get to the gold, until not one stone was left standing upon another.

As ever, the words of Jesus were true, and those that listened saved their lives.

Back to the dispersion of the Jews...

The Jews dispersion had first begun in 586BC when they were carried captive to Babylon, but was completed in 70AD when Rome desolated the city of Jerusalem.

The Jews that remained were dispersed among the nations as Jesus said they would be. It was effectively the end of the Jewish nation.

We can see therefore that history is indeed written beforehand by the all present, all powerful, all knowing God, who is unrestricted by the boundaries of time and space or machinations of man.

Following their dispersal amongst the nations, the Jews suffered the most horrendous persecution, expulsion from nations, the crusades, and worst of all the holocaust. Satan knew that they had to come back to the land for Jesus to return, and because of this he has done all in his power to wipe them off the face of the earth, no matter where they found themselves to be.

However...

The modern day state of Israel is one of the greatest miracles of our day and is in itself profound proof of the utter reliability of Biblical prophecy.

Five Miraculous Fulfilments

1. The Survival of the Jews

When Queen Victoria asked Prime Minister Disraeli, *"What evidence can you give me of the existence of God?"* Disraeli thought for a minute and said *"The Jew your majesty."*

No other people have been scattered across the nations, over such a long period yet retained their identity and come back to their own land. How amazing that through the centuries the Jews have not merged with other nations, despite all their wanderings their clear identity has remained. Many other nations have been lost and merged with others.

When Israel began there were the Jebusites, the Hivites, the Amalekites, many other nations, yet most have never heard of these, yet everyone has heard of the Jews, who were once much smaller than all these other nations.

Many aggressors have sought to wipe out the Jews; the Nazi's for example to name just one.

The battles Israel has come through in modern times show that God has his hand upon them. They won amazing victories against overwhelming odds in both 1948 and 1967, and 1973.

Therefore, the survival of the Jews is a miracle.

2. The Re-establishment of the Nation of Israel

On May 15th 1948 the Nation of Israel was re-established and this fact is a modern day miracle of astounding proportions. Thousands of years ago God gave promises to Abraham and His descendants through Isaac that He has been faithful to:

Ezekiel 36:24-28 *"For I will take you from among the nations, gather you out of all countries, and bring you into your own land. ²⁵Then I will sprinkle clean water on you, and you shall be clean; I will cleanse you from all your filthiness and from all your idols. ²⁶I will give you a new heart and put a new spirit within you; I will take the heart of stone out of your flesh and give you a heart of flesh. ²⁷I will put My Spirit within you and cause you to walk in My statutes, and you will keep My judgements and do them. ²⁸Then you shall dwell in the land that I gave to your fathers; you shall be My people, and I will be your God."*

Nehemiah 1:8 *"Remember, I pray, the word that You commanded Your servant Moses, saying, 'If you are unfaithful, I will scatter you among the* nations; *9but if you return to Me, and keep My commandments and do them, though some of you were cast out to the farthest part of the heavens, yet will gather them from there, and bring them to the place which I have chosen as a dwelling for My name."*

God has a work yet to do among His ancient people the Jews, but their re-gathering is a clear fulfilment of prophesy. The State of Israel stands as a major miracle.

3. The Prosperity of Israel

Israel does not have the massive reserves of oil like its neighbours, yet, even in the worldwide financial crisis it is continuing to enjoy prosperity.

God promised there would be days of prosperity...

Ezekiel 36:10-12 *"I will multiply men upon you, all the house of Israel, all of it; and the cities shall be inhabited and the ruins rebuilt. 11I will multiply upon you man and beast; and they shall increase and bear young; I will make you inhabited as in former times, and do better for you than at your beginnings. Then you shall know that I am the LORD. 12 Yes, I will cause men to walk on you, My people Israel; they shall take possession of you, and you shall be their inheritance; no more shall you bereave them of children."*

Today Israel is one of the world's most prosperous countries. In 1998 Israel had the highest per capita gross domestic product of all the countries around it despite the massive oil incomes of those countries.

Israel's Prosperity is a major miracle.

4. The Agriculture of Israel

God said trees and flowers would grow where they once would not. The land, once barren for centuries has been irrigated, and now Israel exports food to many countries. In recent years over two million trees have been planted.

Isaiah 27:6 *"Those who come He shall cause to take root in Jacob; Israel shall blossom and bud, And fill the face of the world with fruit."*

Isaiah 41:17-20

"I, the God of Israel, will not forsake them.

¹⁸ I will open rivers in desolate heights,
And fountains in the midst of the valleys; I will make the wilderness a pool of water,
And the dry land springs of water.
¹⁹ I will plant in the wilderness the cedar and the acacia tree,
The myrtle and the oil tree;
I will set in the desert the cypress tree and the pine
And the box tree together,
²⁰ That they may see and know,
And consider and understand together,
That the hand of the LORD has done this,
And the Holy One of Israel has created it."

Isaiah 35:1 *"The wilderness and the wasteland shall be glad for them, And the desert shall rejoice and blossom as the rose."*

Today Israel is a major rose exporter.

Israel's prosperity is a sign to the world.

5. Hatred of Israel

It is also a clear fulfilment of God's word that Israel has so many enemies. This nation of Israel has always been surrounded by enemies, and there will come a day when the nations will gather together against them to invade.

Ezekiel refers to the fact that at some point close to the end of the age there will be a great invasion of Israel by a confederation of nations that will look like a great sea. However, just when their annihilation seems certain, God himself will intervene and a great victory will be won against Israel's enemies...

Ezekiel 38:14-17 *"Therefore, son of man, prophesy and say to Gog, 'Thus says the Lord GOD: "On that day when My people Israel dwell safely, will you not know it? ¹⁵ Then you will come from your place out of the far north, you and many people with you, all of them riding on horses, a great company and a mighty army. ¹⁶ You will come up against My people Israel like a cloud, to cover the land. It will be in the latter days that I will bring you against My land, so that the nations may know Me, when I am hallowed in you, O Gog, before their eyes." ¹⁷ Thus says the Lord GOD: "Are you he of whom I have spoken in former days by My servants the prophets* *of Israel, who prophesied for years in those days that I would bring you against them."*

The animosity towards Israel shows us we are in days when the fulfilment of the scriptures could take place at any time. Ezekiel speaks of many nations, some of those names have changed in history as names do. Certainly Russia (the north) and a coalition of Arab countries, Iran (Persia), Eithiopia, Libya, Germany (Gomer) and Turkey.

There are many countries that have publicly declared their aggression to Israel and their desire to see it obliterated. Russia, Iran, and many Islamic nations included.

Despite the Arab Spring we can be certain that this will not lead to a lowering of the aggression against Israel. The probability is that the Muslim hatred of the Jew will increase as the collaboration between Arab nations becomes more unified through bodies such as the Muslim Brotherhood et al and they unite in their desire to see Israel "driven into the sea" as Yasser Arafat once infamously declared. On May 10th in 1996 in a speech in Stockholm, Sweden, Yasser Arafat also said...

"We plan to eliminate the state of Israel and establish a purely Palestinian state. We will make life unbearable for Jews by psychological warfare and population explosion. We Palestinians will take over everything, including all of Jerusalem."

We live in days when an Israeli strike on Iran is imminent. Iran's nuclear potential is soon to be realized and this is an open threat to Israel. Naturally speaking it would seem Israel has little chance, yet God will have the final say. He who made a covenant with Abraham in Genesis 12 also said *"All who bless you (The Jews) I will bless, but those who curse you I will curse."* This has been seen in the outworking of history. The Hatikvah Trust have a well researched documentary series, Israel "Blessing or Curse You can choose." which is recommended viewing.

However, as we have seen...

The fulfilment of God's promises for the Jews concerning their existence, their land, their prosperity, their agriculture, and their lack of popularity are a clear and express sign that God's word always comes to pass.

Isaiah 11:12 *"He will raise a banner for the nations and gather the exiles of*

Israel; he will assemble the scattered people of Judah from the four corners of the earth."

When we read of the things to come, we can be certain they will happen whatever men may feel or say because God is backing up EVERY WORD!

Those who studied prophecy, even those prior to the Balfour declaration of 1917, and the return in 1948 had long predicted Israel must be in the land again before Jesus' return.

Some of the great chronologists (study of Bible dates and times) were remarkable in their predictions of dates concerning this event of re-gathering, taken from Bible prophecy.

One of those brilliant scholars was a man called Dr Robert T Anderson (1842 to 1918). He became an expert on criminal investigation and in 1888 became the head of Scotland Yard. He wrote a number of books on Bible prophecy, and recognised that the Jews needed to return to their homeland before Jesus would return according to the scriptures.

Another writer was Gratton Guinness (1835-1910). He was part of the famous Guinness family. He was a well known preacher and packed halls with eager listeners.

The Dublin Daily Express wrote in 1858:

"Mr Guinness preached yesterday in York Street Chapel. The attendance was greater than any former occasion. In the evening it amounted to 1600, and if there were a place large enough, five times the number would have been present, to hear this highly gifted preacher. The interest which he has excited has daily increased and probably will continue to do so, during his labours in Dublin. An enormous crowd pressed for admittance. Judges, members of Parliament, orators, Fellows of College, lights of the various professions, the rank and fashion of the metropolis have been drawn out. Among them the Lord Lieutenant, the Lord Chancellor and the Lord Justice of Appeal, etc."

His studies led him to recognise that 1917 was a key year for the restoration of the homeland, which he wrote in his book "Light for the Last Days" published in 1888.

In 1917 the Daily Mail reminded readers of Grattan's comments about the importance of the year.

While British troops sought to gain supremacy of the land of Israel General Allenby was appointed Commander in Chief of the Middle East forces. It had been a difficult battle and Allenby was none too pleased at his task. General Beavoir de Lisle noticed the appointment and rushed to see Allenby. He said...

"My dear Allenby, you are on velvet. You may make all the mistakes in tactics or strategy, but nothing will prevent you from being in Jerusalem by the 31st December."

When asked why, he referred to Grattan Guinness, and that Daniel, Ezekiel and Revelation all pointed to 1917.

He also said...

"When you get to Jerusalem, Allenby, I hope you will not ride in state, for that is reserved for one higher than you."

On December 11th as Allenby rode at the head of his troops in victory, he stopped, dismounted his horse and walked into the city of Jerusalem.

Penciled in Grattans notes was the date 1948. On May 14th 1948 Israel officially became a nation again. As God's work spoke so long ago they had come back to their land.

However, though we have given examples of good Biblical scholars above you also need to be careful because...

Some Bible scholars, try to replace Israel with the Church, and state that God has no more plans for Israel and that He has in fact now taken the blessings previously promised to Israel and given them to the Church instead. That feeble argument should have been lost when Israel was reinstated back to their land again. Yet many persist in this foolish delusion much to the delight of the arch deceiver himself, the devil.

However, such teaching is dangerous because it subtly questions and undermines the faithfulness of God to His own promises and word. God made unconditional promises to the Jewish people, and while the church shares in the blessings it can never take their place.

God said Israel would be a banner to the nations. God has backed his word of support to Israel by divine action for THOUSANDS of years.

He will not stop now. Israel is certainly a banner to declare that God is faithful to his word and promises.

There is yet a temple to be rebuilt, the resumption of sacrifice, a peace treaty for seven years.

All these will occur before the Second Advent, but not necessarily before the rapture of the church.

Anyone with an open heart and clear reading of scripture should be able to see that Israel inhabiting their land as a major sign of the near return of Jesus.

What we have learned in this chapter...

- The establishment of Israel promised long ago.

- Its prosperity promised

- Its adversaries aligned as predicted

"The Bible is still loved by millions, read by millions, and studied by millions"

Bernard Ramm

The First And Second Coming of The Lord Jesus Christ

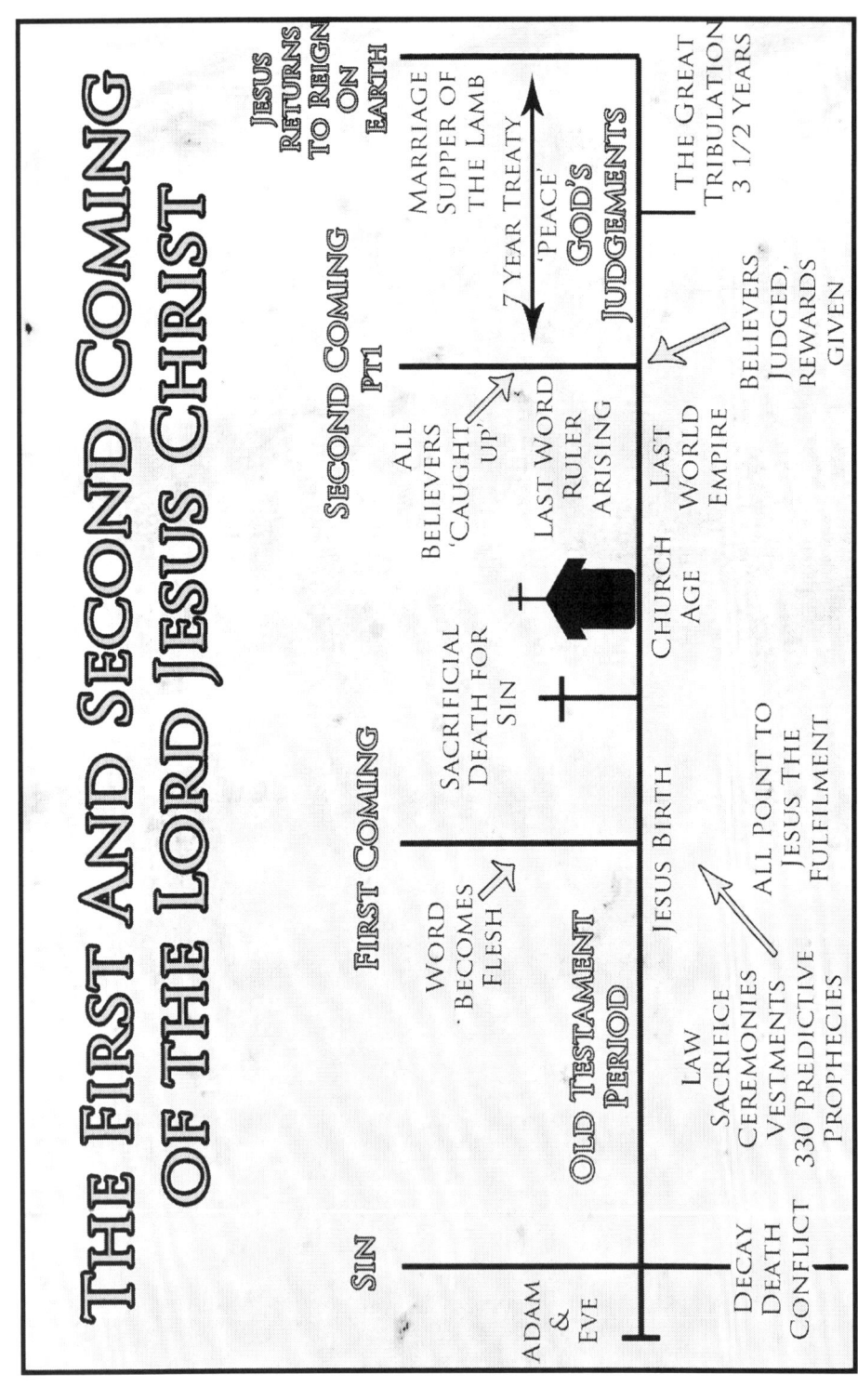

CHAPTER 6

The Second Coming of Christ

Matthew 24:30-31 *"And they will see the Son of Man coming on the clouds of heaven with power and great glory.*[31] *And He will send His angels with a great sound of a trumpet, and they will gather together His elect from the four winds, from one end of heaven to the other."*

The greatest and most awesome event in history is yet to come. While the centre of history has to be the first coming of Jesus Christ, the pinnacle of history will be the most wonderful event of the second coming of the Lord Jesus Christ. All history has been building up to this point, when the flawed and hopeless record of human government will finally come to an end, and the Lord Jesus Christ himself will sit on the throne of the nations.

Only when He the Prince of Peace arrives will the world find true peace.

The devastating effects of man's rejection of God can then be reversed. Ever since Adam and Eve disobeyed God, the power and effect of sin has been evident all around us. Its result is decay and death, sickness and suffering. When Jesus returns He will change everything. Even the creation, glorious in its present condition, will be liberated and far exceed what it is presently.

Romans 8:21*"Because the creation itself also will be delivered from the bondage of corruption into the glorious liberty of the children of God."*

The Bible gives many glimpses of how things will change, there will be a time of peace and God will be the centre of all.

Habakkuk 2:1 *"For the earth will be filled with the knowledge of the glory of the LORD, as the waters cover the sea."*

The first coming of the Lord Jesus was referred to 330 times in the Old Testament; therefore His life was fully documented before He was born. As we have seen, this goes way beyond the law of chance. That all these predictions should be fulfilled so accurately in one person is most certainly beyond chance.

However...

The second coming of Jesus has eight times as many predictions as the first coming. He who came once is surely coming back again, this time not humble, meek and mild as a servant, but to reign over the nations.

There will only be one criteria when the Lord Jesus returns, only one thing that can enable us to stand before Him. You must be one of those whose names are written in the Lamb's Book of Life (Revelation 20:15) have been submitted to Him and has repented of their sins and believed the gospel. Only these people will be able to stand and later be accepted into heaven.

Concerning the second coming, the Apostle Peter warns us that there will be cynical and unbelieving people who will mock that such a thing will even occur...

2 Peter 3:2-3 *"That you may be mindful of the words spoken before by the holy prophets, and the commandments of us the apostles of our lord and saviour, knowing this first that scoffers will come in the last days saying where is the promise of his coming for since the fathers fell asleep all things continue just as they were from the beginning of creation."*

Yes, people may mock, but the day is coming soon when each will see with their own eyes the truthfulness of God's promises.

At the time of Jesus assumption into heaven, the angel declared in Acts 1:9-11... *"This same Jesus, who was taken up from you into heaven, will so come in like manner as you saw Him go into heaven."*

Two Parts

The second coming will be fulfilled in not one, but two separate events.

When Jesus came the first time the Jews expected all the prophecies concerning the Messiah to be fulfilled in one event. In the Old Testament the coming Messiah was referred to as the suffering servant (Isaiah 53) and also in many places as the coming king of the nations (Zechariah 14).

The Jews did not differentiate between these two roles, yet when He came Jesus made it clear that He would also come again, a second time, when the outstanding prophecies concerning Him would then be fulfilled. For the Jew at the time this had been hard to see, for us looking back it is easy. I am sure after Jesus has returned, there will be things we did not understand clearly, but then we will look back and realise it had all been written beforehand.

Likewise, when Jesus comes the second time there will be two stages, a coming for His people, and a coming back to earth to reign. These are clearly different events, but both come under the banner of the second coming.

Part 1

The first event of the second coming will be the catching up of the "bride of Christ" which is the church. It is important to understand that the church is not an organisation or denomination, but the church from God's viewpoint consists of all who have put their faith in Jesus' sacrifice for them on the cross, the saints of God.

1 Thessalonians 4:15-17 *"We who are alive and remain until the coming of the Lord will by no means precede those who have fallen asleep, ¹⁶ for the Lord himself will descend from heaven with the voice of the archangel, and the trump of God, the dead in Christ shall rise first, ¹⁷ then we who are alive and remain shall be caught up together with them to meet the Lord in the air. Thus shall we ever be with the Lord."*

The Lord is coming first for His people. Vitally, this will not be a public event where Christ comes in the clouds and every eye sees Him, it will be an event for believers only.

It comes, I believe before the terrible days of the last seven years. These last seven years of world history will be a horrific time, when God will finally act after having waited so long, to judge the world and all in it for their wilful rebellion against Him.

Just as God saved Lot from the fire, when he judged Sodom and Gomorrah, and Noah from the great flood, God's plan is to remove His people (those who love Him above all else) before the terrible events of the last days of this age. God does not intend to pour His judgement out upon those who have looked to the cross of Jesus and been saved by His precious blood.

This first stage is called the rapture of the church; when all who believe will receive new immortal bodies.

1 Corinthians 15:51-52 *"Behold, I tell you a mystery: We shall not all sleep, but we shall all be changed [52] in a moment, in the twinkling of an eye, at the last trumpet. For the trumpet will sound, and the dead will be raised incorruptible, and we shall be changed."*

How wonderful it will be to live in a new immortal body, no more sickness or fatigue, but eternal life in the presence of God!

Luke 21:36 *"Watch therefore, and pray always that you may be counted worthy to escape all these things that will come to pass and to stand before the Son of Man."*

Time of Christ's Return?

There are various viewpoints on the timing of the first stage of the second coming, the "rapture", but what matters is whether we are ready and can be part of it when it does occur.

In fact...

We can begin to get ready and continue to live ready beginning right now!

Regardless of our belief on the timing of the rapture we cannot discount the fact that we may have difficult days ahead. Large parts of the world already suffer greatly for their faith, and there are worrying trends emerging in the United Kingdom and European law at this time.

For the first time in history the ancient institution of marriage is being challenged by the British government. Their aim is for same sex marriage. God himself declares this is sinful and His word is final. To challenge God is a dangerous thing.

Christianity is being marginalised. Recently cases have reached the European courts, where the wearing of a cross has been forbidden, and also where a hotel refused a room to a gay couple resulted in a judgement against the Christian hotel owners making their action "criminal".

There have also been arrests of those peacefully demonstrating against abortion. In one sense the day of free speech is already over because if you speak God's word concerning these things you are likely to suffer severe consequences from both society and government alike, united in their opposition to Biblical guidelines for holy living.

We are, however, privileged in the Western world not to be under the vicious persecution faced in areas of China, North Korea and the Islamic world. People are daily being martyred for their faith in the Lord Jesus.

So the blood of the martyrs is flowing now even as we speak, but the rapture is approaching too. And it will come SUDDENLY.

This sudden catching away of Christians will take the world by surprise. Millions will disappear overnight. To explain it the world may be told this was an "alien abduction" or a "cleansing of the earth by Mother Nature, of those narrow minded fundamentalist Christians".

There will be those left behind that have heard the gospel, but not believed it or have put off responding. Many will now respond as they suddenly realise all they had previously learned about Jesus and the end times was true. They will face a difficult time on earth that God never intended for Christians to face because He loves His own deeply. Nevertheless they will be able to come to the Lord Jesus, and be assured of their eternal salvation despite having to go through this time of great tribulation.

When Jesus has come for the believers they will go to heaven first to be judged for their works while on earth. This is not a judgement for sin, but a special appraisal of the believers work. Concerning this the Bible reveals there will be rewards for those who have faithfully served Him...

1 Corinthians 3:11-15 *"For no other foundation can anyone lay than that which is laid, which is Jesus Christ. ¹² Now if anyone builds on this*

foundation with gold, silver, precious stones, wood, hay, straw, [13] each one's work will become clear; for the Day will declare it, because it will be revealed by fire; and the fire will test each one's work, of what sort it is. [14] If anyone's work which he has built on it endures, he will receive a reward. [15] If anyone's work is burned, he will suffer loss; but he himself will be saved, yet so as through fire."

For all there will be some regrets, yet for some this will be a time of great regret, realising that the gifts, talents, abilities and possessions that were entrusted to them by God were wasted. How important it is to make the best of every day as an opportunity to serve God and to obey Jesus' words. Matthew 25:14 -30 makes it clear we will be rewarded accordingly.

Life is so short, but while we are here we have an opportunity to be a blessing to those around us. Sharing the good news of Jesus Christ in both word and deed can make such a difference.

Part Two

The second stage of the second coming will be a public appearance of Jesus, where every eye will see Christ. This will be after the time of great tribulation. Jesus will be coming back as the King of Kings and Lord of Lords.

Jesus Himself will sit upon the throne of the nations, in fulfilment of the promises of God, as we are told in...

Revelation 19:11-16 *"And I saw heaven opened, and behold a white horse. And He who sat upon it was called Faithful and True, and in righteousness He judges and makes war. [12] His eyes were like a flame of fire, and on His head were many crowns. He had a name written that no one knew except Himself. [13] He was clothed with a robe dipped in blood, and His name is called the word of God. [14] And the armies in heaven, clothed in fine linen, white and clean, followed Him on white horses. [15] Now out of His mouth goes a sharp two edged sword that with it He shall strike the nations. And He Himself shall rule them with a rod of iron. He Himself treads the winepress of the fierceness and wrath of Almighty God. [16] And He has on His robe and on His thigh a name written* **King of Kings and Lord of Lords.***"*

The passages concerning Jesus' public revealing make it clear that He is coming back, not this time as the suffering servant, as the first time, but as the King to reign.

Daniel 7:13-14 says...

"I was watching in the night visions,
And behold, One like the Son of Man,
Coming with the clouds of heaven!
He came to the Ancient of Days,
And they brought Him near before Him.
¹⁴ Then to Him was given dominion and glory and a kingdom,
That all peoples, nations, and languages should serve Him.
His dominion is an everlasting dominion,
Which shall not pass away,
And His kingdom the one
Which shall not be destroyed.

The angel Gabriel also makes it clear when he announces the coming of Jesus in Luke 1:32-33... *"He shall be great, and shall be called the son of the Highest and the Lord God will give Him the throne of His father David. ³³ And He shall reign over the house of Jacob forever, and of His kingdom there shall be no end."*

So...

We who have received Jesus as our Lord and Saviour and been forgiven our sins are going to be raptured, taken up in the air, in an instant to be with Him. There will be a judgement of our works. Those who become Christians after the rapture will join the rest in heaven, though they have to pass through the tribulation. What a wonderful time of reunion there will be. The church will be together, past and present with all of God's people through the ages.

In Jude we read of an ancient prophecy by Enoch...

Jude 1:14 *"Now Enoch, the seventh from Adam, prophesies about these men also, saying, 'Behold the Lord comes with ten thousands of his saints, to execute judgement upon all.' "*

From this it seems that raptured believers may have an exciting role to play in the second coming too. They will be returning to earth with the Lord Jesus and even play a part in executing God's judgement at that stage. Truly God is just, and how fitting it will be that we as His sons and daughters will join with the most just judge of all and execute His judgements against all the injustices that have been perpetrated throughout the earth. God is so good!

A wonderful day is coming soon when the reign of man on earth will be over, and God himself will set up His Kingdom, and we are offered a part. Through God's sacrifice of His Son we can all enjoy a part in this glorious future when the earth will enjoy true justice and leadership.

As we have seen in the World Leader chapter, the world will be returned to its rightful owner and the kingdoms of this world will become the kingdoms of our God and of His Christ.

The second coming of Jesus is a key doctrine of the Bible, but as Peter warned in his letter, belief has waned and many are cynical of this. However, as we look out at the world scene and the fulfilment of prophecy, we see everything lines up perfectly with this doctrine. The stage is being set today for these events to take place very shortly.

Jesus spoke a number of parables about His return; the main theme of these was that we should be ready for His return. He warned there would be those caught by surprise, unprepared, and those who would be found unfaithful. If you are not ready, then you need to be. Please turn to the last chapter of this book now and find out how.

In the light of end time events Jesus told us not to just sit back and wait. In the parable of the ten talents the master said, 'occupy till I come.' He says the same to us. As long as we are here on earth we have a job to do. The great job of the Church, all believers, is to obey the Great Commission of Jesus in Matthew 28:18-20...

"And Jesus came and spake unto them, saying, 'All power is given unto me in heaven and in earth. [19] Go ye therefore, and teach all nations, baptising them in the name of the Father, and of the Son, and of the Holy Ghost: [20]Teaching them to observe all things whatsoever I have commanded you: and, lo, I am with you always, even unto the end of the world. Amen.' "

This is so important. God will give people every opportunity to hear His truth through each of us, as we share about Him with others before He returns. We have been given a challenging yet privileged role. His will is for all to be saved, though not all will be. We cannot of ourselves convert people; we can only give them the message, and leave the rest to God.

2 Peter 3:9 *"The Lord is not slack concerning his promise, as some men count slackness; but is long suffering to us-ward, not willing that any should perish, but that all should come to repentance."*

God has a master plan of history. It culminates with the most glorious event that the world itself is waiting for. Jesus is coming soon!

In this chapter we have learned...

- Jesus' second coming is imminent

- It will be in two stages

- Only believers will be taken up

- There will be a judgement of works, and rewards given

"To the BIBLE men will return; and why? Because they cannot do without it."

Matthew Arnold

SEVENTY WEEKS 70X7 490 YEARS

69 WEEKS

DECREE TO REBUILD CITY AND

ARTEXERCES MARCH 14TH 445BC

PUBLIC DECLARATION OF JESUS AS MESSIAH

TRIUMPHAL ENTRY TO JERUSALEM APRIL 6TH 32AD

MESSIAH CUT OFF

DESTRUCTION OF JERUSALEM

ISRAEL ESTABLISHED AS A NATION

GAP

ANTI-CHRIST

MARK OF THE BEAST

GREAT TRIBULATION

1 WEEK

PEACE AGREEMENT, MIDDLE EAST 7 YEARS

CHAPTER 7

Daniel's Seventy Weeks

"*The BIBLE is not merely a book; it is a Living being, with an action, a power, which invades everything that opposes its extension, behold! It is upon this table this Book, surpassing all others; I never omit to read it, and every day with some pleasure.*" (Napoleon Bonaparte)

In this chapter I want to focus on one portion of prophecy that is particularly amazing in its fulfilment. Its remarkable accuracy speaks of the integrity of the Word of God and wakes us up to the dramatic events, which are preparing our world, not for the end of time, but for the end of this present age. God has yet a wonderful plan for the future. There are ages yet to come. This present age will close and a new one will begin with the return of Jesus.

What we are discussing here therefore, is something that many seem to miss, even those who speak concerning the End Time. We are not merely discussing the end times, we are more accurately discussing the close of one age and the opening of another far better one, planned in the heart of God from the very beginning.

Now onto Daniel...

At the time of writing Daniel the prophet was living in the Persian Empire, and had recently escaped the lion's den. It was while he was in prayer for his nation and his people that he was interrupted by none other than the angel Gabriel, who seems to appear throughout scripture specifically in relation to the coming of the promised Messiah. (See also Luke 1:26-33)

The word translated into "weeks" in this following passage does not have a tight, specific definition in the original Hebrew text as the word "weeks" is understood in today's English. It can actually count as any period of seven. To the Jews this was perfectly normal; they had weeks of days, weeks of weeks, and weeks of years. Given the context of the passage in Daniel, this use of 'weeks' is clearly referring to weeks of years. In other words the angel Gabriel was relaying a message concerning a 490 year period.

This is VERY important to understand as you will see.

The seventieth week or last seven years is a subject by itself, which we will touch on later. We will start with the sixty nine weeks first.

Here is our passage...

Daniel 9:24-27

"Seventy weeks are determined for your people and for your holy city. To finish the transgression, to make an end of sins. To make reconciliation for iniquity. To bring in everlasting righteousness. To seal up vision and prophecy and to anoint the most holy.

[25] Know therefore that from the going forth of the command to restore and rebuild Jerusalem, until Messiah the prince, there will be seven weeks and sixty two weeks. The street shall be built again, even the wall in troublesome times.

[26] After sixty two weeks the Messiah will be cut off but not for Himself. The people of the prince who is to come will destroy the city and the sanctuary. The end of it shall be with a flood. And until the end of the war desolations are determined.

[27] Then he shall confirm a covenant with the many for one week, but in the middle of the week he shall bring an end to sacrifice and offering. And on the wings of abomination shall be one who makes desolate. Even until the consummation which is determined is poured out on the desolate."

This prophecy is amazing in its detail. Its existence long before any of its fulfilment is solidly established, because it was contained in the Septuagint translation of the Old Testament way back in 270BC.

We are studying the first sixty nine weeks, a 483 year period. At the end of sixty nine weeks the Messiah will be declared as who He is, and then the scripture says He will be cut off for the people, which is a clear reference to the sacrificial death of Jesus on the cross.

How amazingly accurate!

The Three Decrees

The start point of our prophetic period is the decree to rebuild the city and the wall. There were three decrees so it is vital to get our start point fixed. It is a matter of fact that the city and the wall were rebuilt in history.

There are four decrees, three of which are noted in the book of Ezra.

The first decree is by King Cyrus and concerns the building of the temple.

This contains no mention of the walls and is therefore not right. (To fit the prophecy the decree must deal with both the street and the wall).

Ezra 1:2-4 documents the decree of King Cyrus.

The second decree is in Ezra 6 and 8 and is the decree of King Darius.

The third is the decree of King Artaxerxes in Ezra 7.

None of these three references deal with the "street and the wall" and therefore cannot be the reference start point of Daniel's prophecy.

And the forth is the decree of Artaxerxes in Nehemiah 2. It is this last decree alone that deals with the rebuilding of the city as well as the temple, and therefore this is the only one that fits.

Thanks to the studious and well respected works of Sir Robert Anderson published in 1894, (The Coming Prince), we can safely date this event as March 14th 445BC. This allows for changes in calendars etc. This date is obtained from the details included in the text, and the date of Arterxerxes' reign which is widely agreed by secular historians and chronologists.

So from this date we are looking at 483 years until Messiah the Prince.

The context of the prophecy is particularly the city of Jerusalem. The day of the Messiah being revealed publicly was an exact day that can be pinpointed, and occurred in Jerusalem.

Throughout his ministry Jesus had referred to His Messiah-ship only in veiled terms for those who had ears to hear, but had deliberately withheld from any public announcements.

In Matthew 16:20, following Peter's recognition that Jesus is the Messiah the Gospel passage says... *"Then He commanded His disciples that they should tell no one that He was Jesus the Christ."*

However, when Jesus was here on earth during His first coming, there was a day when He clearly and publicly declared that He was in fact the long awaited Messiah. He also mourns the fact that the people do not realise that this is in fact the day of their "visitation".

Luke 19:44b *"They will not leave one stone upon another because you did not know the time of your visitation."*

We read the account of Jesus' triumphal entry into Jerusalem on the day we call Palm Sunday.

Luke 19:30 *"Everything was in place; the colt was there just as Jesus said it would be."*

This was a day ordained before history began, and was to be a definite revealing of the Messiah during Jesus' first visit to earth.

In Luke 13:34 Jesus wept over Jerusalem and its history... *"I say unto you shall not see me until the time comes when you say "Blessed is he who comes in the name of the Lord."* (Quoting Psalm 118:26)

This will be a very significant time for Jerusalem. The words Jesus declares in advance are from Psalm 118. As this was the time of Passover the words of Psalm 118 were always read. This is THE day the Psalm spoke of in advance, and declared... *"This is the day the Lord has made; I will rejoice and be glad in it."*

This Psalm is full of references to the coming Messiah. When these words were spoken out by the people to Jesus they were making a proclamation of who they believed He was, ie., the very Messiah Himself, hence we read the Pharisees were very angry.

Let's look at the triumphal entry into Jerusalem...

Luke 19:37-39 *"Then as He was now drawing near the descent of the mount of olives, the whole multitude of the disciples began to rejoice and praise God with a loud voice for all the mighty works they had seen, [38] saying "Blessed is the King who comes in the name of the Lord! Peace in the highest heaven and glory in the highest." [39] And some of the Pharisees called to Him from the crowd "Teacher, rebuke your disciples."*

The Pharisees were upset because they realised the significance of these words from Psalm 118 - that they were a specific response recognising Jesus as the Messiah.

This very day, planned by God from eternity past, when Jesus was publicly declared as Messiah the King was the very day the angel Gabriel spoke of to Daniel 483 years beforehand.

Many things point to Jesus' Messiah-ship being revealed as the Messiah at this point. It is not insignificant that He rode on a donkey that had been tethered.

Genesis 49:10-11 *"The sceptre will not depart from Judah, nor the ruler's staff from between his feet, until he comes to whom it belongs and the obedience of the nations is his. [11] He will tether his donkey to a vine, His colt to the choicest branch. He will wash His garments in wine, His robes in the blood of grapes."*

The sceptre refers to kingship, and it was predicted that the Messiah would come from the tribe of Judah, the royal line. This ancient prophecy referred to the Messiah coming, and linked it to the donkey which He rode into Jerusalem.

We are told specifically no one else had ridden on this donkey. If an animal was being kept for royal or sacred purposes this would always be the case.

As in 2 Kings 9:13 the throwing down of cloaks was a recognition of royalty.

Very significantly, Jesus not only accepted the praise, but encouraged it declaring that the very stones would cry out if the people did not.

So from our beginning point at the command to rebuild the city and the sanctuary, we have our end point when Jesus not only declared Himself as the Messiah, but then went on to be "cut off" for the people by His sacrificial death on the cross in Jerusalem.

Thanks to the meticulous work of Dr Robert Anderson we can confidently affirm this was April 6th 32AD. This is ascertained from the beginning point of Luke's statement that Jesus' public ministry began in the fifteenth year of Tiberius, and taken to the date of the Passover in 32AD.

So from our beginning point to the end point we have two clear dates.

From the issuing of the command to rebuild the city and the wall was indeed sixty nine weeks of years, 483 years, 173880 days. What an amazing miracle, beyond any possibility of chance that on the exact day Gabriel spoke of, the Messiah should declare himself to Israel.

So...

We can see that in history so far, sixty nine weeks have already passed, and the predictions made concerning them have proved astonishingly credible. Therefore we can rest assured that the rest of this prophecy will also come to pass with similar stunning accuracy.

Following the sixty ninth week there is clearly a gap. This is not unusual in prophecy. A similar example of this type of prophetic 'gap' may be seen when Jesus quotes Isaiah 61 whilst in the synagogue. He only gives half of the prophesy, the part he declares fulfilled; the rest is yet to come.

Luke 4:18-20 *"The Spirit of the Lord is upon me, because he hath anointed me to preach the gospel to the poor; he hath sent me to heal the broken hearted, to preach deliverance to the captives, and recovering of sight to the blind, to set at liberty them that are bruised, ^{19} To preach the acceptable year of the Lord. ^{20} And he closed the book."*

Another example is on the day of Pentecost, Peter quotes Joel 2. He gives only the start of the prophecy, the part being fulfilled, but leaves the next part unspoken because it is yet to be fulfilled.

In Daniel 9 there is a gap between the sixty nine weeks and the seventieth week.

This is clear because the prophecy details that the Messiah will be cut off. The word for cut off in the original Hebrew text means executed, which is exactly what happened to Jesus. His execution was not for Himself, but rather for you and I and the whole of the world.

Next in Daniel we read that the people of the prince who is to come will destroy the temple. That did not happen until 70AD, and clearly happened in a gap between the sixty ninth and seventieth week. Therefore it is clear that the seventieth week has not yet started and is still in the future.

This seventieth week will be the last week of present history; it will begin when the world leader, a Roman prince signs a peace treaty. He will break this after 3 and 1/2 years, abolish Jewish sacrifices which will be happening again, and will set up the "abomination of desolation." Jesus referred to this in...

Matthew 24:15-16 *"Therefore when you see the abomination of desolation spoken of by Daniel the prophet standing in the Holy place, [16] then let those who are in Judea flee to the mountains."*

Like many key events in prophecy, they are also prefigured beforehand in history, almost as "pre-prophecies" which serve to double underline that there will be a later, complete fulfilment of the scriptural promise.

One example is Antiochus Epiphanes who was a Seleucid King. His life and death were miraculously detailed in Daniel 11. He slaughtered a pig (an unclean animal to Jews) in the Temple, and set up an image of Zeus in the Holy of Holies. This fulfilled the term "abomination of desolation" used for the later time when the Anti-Christ will set up his image (in a similar way to how Antiochus set up the image Zeus in the Holy of Holies) to be worshipped.

Jesus, in his Olivet discourse of events marking His coming and the end of the age, makes this reference to Daniel. He identifies Daniel as a prophet, and takes his words literally.

Daniel himself could have no knowledge of what was to come, but the God of heaven whom he served is indeed a revealer of secrets. How strange that vague prophecies from the likes of Nostradamus, astrologers and others have such wide exposure today, yet such clear and lucid prophecies from the Bible are almost unheard of?

In this chapter we have learned...

- Daniel 9 is a key to understanding the end of history

- God gave to Daniel details of the exact day when Jesus would ride into Jerusalem on the donkey, 483 years before it actually happened

- We are living in the gap between the sixty ninth and seventieth week of years

- The last week will begin with the Anti-Christ signing a peace treaty

- The Antichrist will set up his own image in a restored Jewish temple

- When the seventieth week starts there will only be seven (normal, current) left of this age

"The BIBLE -- banned, burned, beloved. More widely read, more frequently attacked than any other book in history. Generations of intellectuals have attempted to discredit it, dictators of every age have outlawed it and executed those who read it. Yet soldiers carry it into battle believing it more powerful than their weapons. Fragments of it smuggled into solitary prison cells have transformed ruthless killers into gentle saints"

Charles Colson

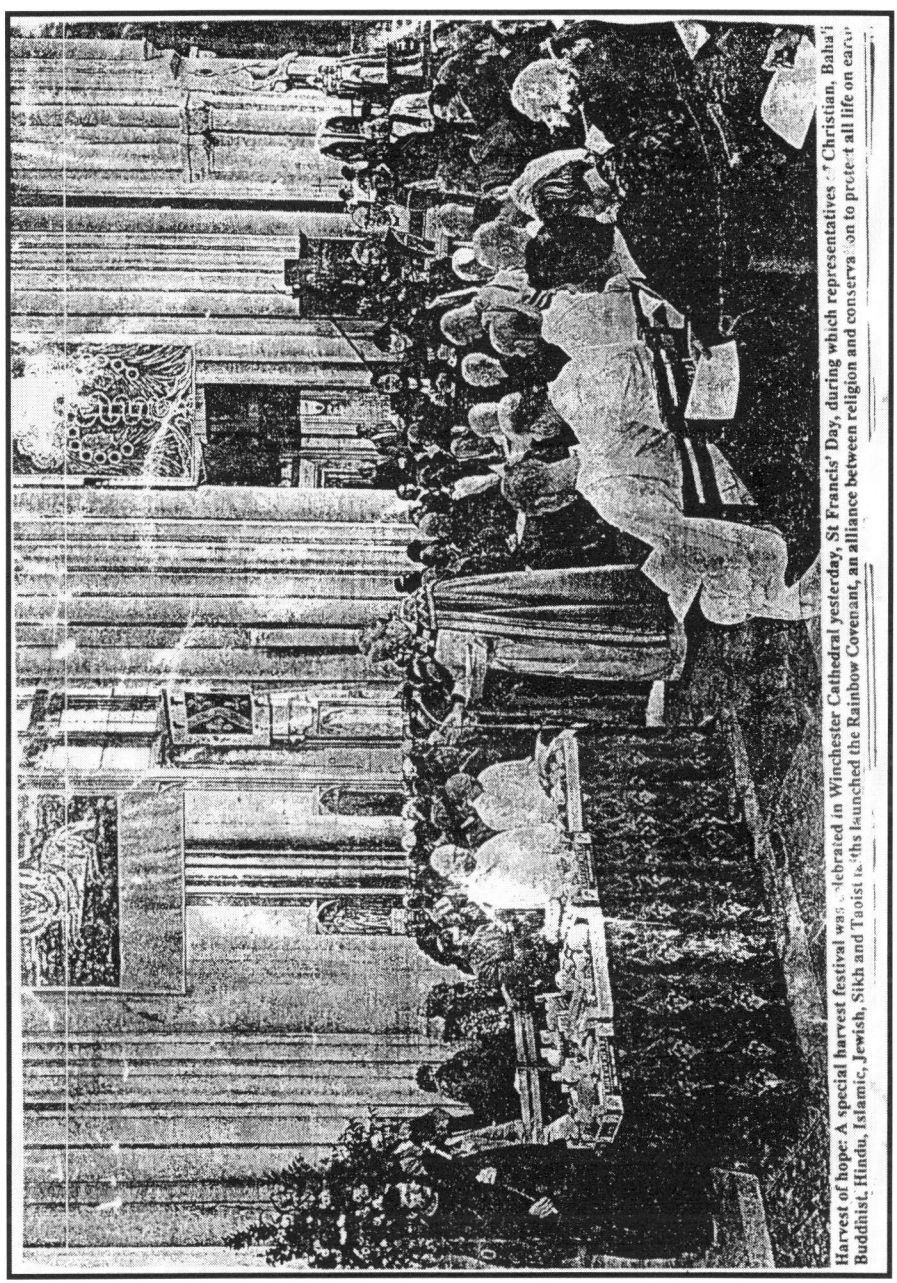

Harvest of hope: A special harvest festival was celebrated in Winchester Cathedral yesterday, St Francis' Day, during which representatives of Christian, Baha'i, Buddhist, Hindu, Islamic, Jewish, Sikh and Taoist faiths launched the Rainbow Covenant, an alliance between religion and conservation to protect all life on earth

CHAPTER 8
Global Deceptions

A Global Deception is underway...

The first warning Jesus gave concerning the end of the age was that there would be false Christs who would deceive many. This is certainly the case today, with many proclaiming themselves as Guru's and spiritual teachers.

The world is being prepared spiritually to receive a false messiah through an aversion to absolute truth, and a rejection of the basic Biblical standards that have previously been the backbone of wholesome society. With an emphasis on stopping discrimination and hate crime, which is important, there is a danger that new laws can easily be twisted to stop anything seen as a criticism of another lifestyle. The Bible clearly teaches right and wrong, because life is rudderless without a strong moral framework. The Ten Commandments have proven to be a wonderful framework for a successful and happy society.

God in His wisdom made a great variety of people, and while we may not agree on everything together, the world would be a boring place if everyone was a clone of each other. It is important people can express views whether right or wrong, lest the day come, when Christianity is considered wrong and we are not allowed to speak.

In this post modern age absolute truth is frowned upon, and truth has become abstract. It is now whatever you want it to be. Spirituality is fashionable but Christianity is not.

These sort of teachings are dangerous because...

Truth is definite and subjective; a belief is either true or not. However much we believe something our belief cannot make it true. Once people believed sincerely that the earth was flat, but all of their belief did not create what they believed - they were just wrong.

Occult Resurgence

Part of the preparation to receive the Anti-Christ is through the acceptance of occult practices. The Bible warned from early in history that occult practices were to be shunned. When God speaks in such strong terms there is always a good reason. These practices open people and society up to spiritual infiltration from the powers of darkness, in turn preparing people to accept the Anti-Christ. We are warned the last days would be like the days of Noah. In those days there was excessive occultism and forbidden practices.

Deuteronomy 18:9-14

"When you come into the land which the LORD your God is giving you, you shall not learn to follow the abominations of those nations. [10] There shall not be found among you anyone who makes his son or his daughter pass through the fire, or one, who practices witchcraft, or a soothsayer, or one who interprets omens, or a sorcerer, [11] or one who conjures spells, or a medium, or a spiritist, or one who calls up the dead. [12] For all who do these things are an abomination to the LORD, and because of these abominations the LORD your God drives them out from before you. [13] You shall be blameless before the LORD your God. [14] For these nations which you will dispossess listened to soothsayers and diviners; but as for you, the LORD your God has not appointed such for you."

A recent Barna survey showed around 75% of American youth had dabbled in the occult. Recent films such as the Harry Potter series have inspired a renewed interest in witchcraft and occultism.

While to many Spiritual Healers, Psychic, Fortune tellers and Ouija boards are just harmless fun, they are dabbling with danger, which cannot only damage them, but cause them serious spiritual problems.

Even the Vatican has held a conference on exorcism (expulsion of evil spirits) because it is concerned with how rapidly interest in the occult is growing.

A six-day exorcism conference in Rome attracted sixty Catholic clergy including doctors, psychologists, psychiatrists, teachers and youth workers to talk about how to deal with devil worship.

Carlo Climati who is a writer and employee of the Vatican's Regina Apostolorum Pontifical University, specialising in the dangers posed to young people by Satanism hosted the conference. He thinks that Satanism is on the rise thanks to the Internet.

"The internet makes it much easier than in the past to find information about Satanism," said Climati *"In just a few minutes you can contact Satanist groups and research occultism. The conference is not about how to become an exorcist. It's to share information about exorcism, Satanism and sects. It's to give help to families and priests. There is a particular risk for young people who are in difficulties or who are emotionally fragile,"* (The Daily Telegraph)

Satan is the great deceiver, and is described by Paul as the god of this world.

2 Corinthians 4:4 *"Whose minds the god of this age has blinded, who do not believe, lest the light of the gospel of the glory of Christ, who is the image of God, should shine on them."*

Jesus said of him in John 8:44-45...

"You are of your father the devil, and the desires of your father you want to do. He was a murderer from the beginning, and does not stand in the truth, because there is no truth in him. When he speaks a lie, he speaks from his own resources, for he is a liar and the father of it. [45] But because I tell the truth, you do not believe Me."

The work of Satan is about deceiving people; he uses some truth, but also mixes it with error. A counterfeit has to look like the real thing to fool anyone, and with knowledge of the Bible at low ebb many people are easily fooled into accepting something "spiritual" as being truth.

Speaking to the dead is a perfect example...

People are deceived into thinking they are speaking to a departed loved one because what the Bible terms as familiar spirits that followed a person when alive, masquerade as that person (during a séance for example), revealing information about a loved one that only the dead person could have known. Therefore, gullible grieving relatives are taken in and hooked by this information. God did not say occult techniques never work, He simply said not to do them. Many people feel that if something is supernatural it must be okay. Nothing could be further from the truth.

2 Thessalonians 2:9-10 *"The coming of the lawless one is according to the working of Satan, with all power, signs, and lying wonders, ¹⁰ and with all unrighteous deception among those who perish, because they did not receive the love of the truth, that they might be saved."*

This global surge in the rise of the occult is one of the many signs of the coming of the end, and a tactic of Satan to prepare people to receive the False Christ.

The Origin of Satan

When Jesus referred to Satan as a liar from the beginning he was referring to the Garden of Eden, where he lied to Adam and Eve.

But who is this being, Satan, who appeared in Eden?

In Ezekiel 28 and Isaiah 14 the Bible reveals his origins. He was an angel created by God, a cherubim, glorious in beauty and elevated in position. However, he became full of pride and wanted to be god himself. Because of his sin he was cast out of heaven. He had already gossiped and caused undercurrents among the angels and managed to sway a third of the multitudes of angels to side with him in his rebellion.

Since then Satan and his angels have been doing all in their power to turn people against God, and convince them God is not real. Occult beliefs, other religions, cults, all are inspired by satanic forces. Like all of Satan's works they do not bring freedom and liberty as Jesus came to do, but enslavement and misery. The whole aim is to keep people from the wonderful freedom they can experience in knowing God.

Jesus said in John 8:31-32... *"Then Jesus said to those Jews who believed Him, 'If you abide in My word, you are My disciples indeed. ³² And you shall know the truth, and the truth shall make you free.'"*

The Two Lies

In the Garden of Eden Satan came. His aim was to deceive Adam and

Eve. God had ruled out only one item as forbidden in all the glories of Paradise, the tree of the knowledge of good and evil. That tree represented choice, for without choice there is no freedom. The tree also spoke of man's autonomy, God wanted Adam and Eve to trust him and walk with him. He didn't want them to have knowledge of evil.

God's warning was clear,

Genesis 2:16-17 *"Of every tree of the garden you may freely eat; ¹⁷ but of the tree of the knowledge of good and evil you shall not eat, for in the day that you eat of it you shall surely die."*

The devil, as he always does, tried to get them to question that word…

Genesis 3:4-5 *"You will not surely die. ⁵ For God knows that in the day you eat of it your eyes will be opened and you will be like God, knowing good and evil."*

These two lies have been the basis for many false beliefs ever since. Satan the god of this world is a deceiver. His plan is to undermine the clear truths of God's word and to implement false beliefs that cause people to believe that they do not need God.

1. You shall not die

The first comment - you shall not surely die - should have been seen forever as false following the death of every person through history, none have not died. Yet in his subtlety this lie has continued in the new age ideas of reincarnation and karma, that life is a continuing cycle.

Yet God makes it very clear that reincarnation, for example, is false and that all shall die once…

Hebrews 9:27 *"And as it is appointed for men to die once, but after this the judgement,"*

It is also fascinating that people so often close their minds to death. They spend their lives preparing and caring for their needs for their short span; yet neglect their needs for all eternity.

2. The second lie, you shall be as God.

This has come through to New Age doctrine that suggests we are gods, and that we have an infinite potential that we only have to realise in order to enter this "higher state of god-like being and consciousness". This is in contrast with God's truth, that man is a sinner by nature, and only through receiving the Lord Jesus and being born again can he be made good because only then he can accept the royal exchange Jesus affected for us at the Cross through His death and resurrection.

It is only through this "royal exchange" that we qualify to accept His wonderful goodness and resurrection life in exchange (through repentance) for our old sin corrupted natures, in order to live in harmony with God enjoying the brand new nature Jesus then gives us.

History gives a clear picture that man is ultimately corrupt. Many people believe in the innate goodness of man, yet again such thinking is illogical. This belief is of course part of Satan's aim to undermine belief in the true and living God, and ultimately try to overthrow His dominion, which of course is futile on his part because God is omnipotent, omniscient and omnipresent.

Lies in Our Education

Satan's career is one of lies. Perhaps one of the most destructive of those lies has been the promotion of the theory of evolution. History shows this has been a key issue in turning people away from a belief in God and the Bible. It has been promoted as a fact rather than a theory, and even though there are more and more discoveries that prove evolution as a flawed theory it continues to be taught as fact. These discoveries include the tremendous complexity of the human DNA. There are numerous good books on the subject - Sylvia Baker MSc "Bone of Contention, Is Evolution True?" is a good starting point. "Answers in Genesis" have an excellent website and a wide range of material available.

Many of the discoveries that are used to teach evolution have been proven to be fraudulent such as pictures of embryos from different animals drawn by Ernst Haeckel in the 19th century.

This is how evolutionists claim in their ontogenesis argument that we all evolved from the same organism. This fraud was discovered more than 100 years ago and yet is still in our textbooks. If you simply Google Ernst Haeckel you will quickly discover all the proof you need to see this fraud for what it is.

- Nebraska man was a fraud based on a single tooth of a rare type of pig

- Java man was based on weak evidence of a femur, skull cap and three teeth found within a wide area over a one year period. It turns out the bones were found in an area of human remains, and now the femur is considered human and the skull cap from a large ape.

- Neanderthal man was traditionally depicted as a stooped ape-man. It is now accepted that the ape's posture was due to disease and that Neanderthal is just a variation of the human.

Some examples years later still appear in text books. If we cannot believe the initial chapters of the Bible we cannot believe any of it. While micro evolution-adaptation to environment is a fact, there is no clear evidence for evolution of one species to another. There is not room here to deal with this issue, but it is a key issue in our day and we could like to point you to the work of 'Answers in Genesis' and 'Creation Science' to find out more.

One of the greatest evidences for creation is the intricacy of the creation. The absolutely incredible detail of nature is the work of a mastermind. Latest research in the DNA has also revealed incredible intricacies in the make-up of the human cell that even our latest technology could not begin to mimic.

All of Satan's lies are aimed at discrediting God's word and keeping people away from the truth.

Deception in the Church

The church has not been immune from deception. Many of the letters in the New Testament are aimed at maintaining doctrinal purity. Yet it is sad that the rise of higher criticism brought Satan's lies into the heart of the church. Higher criticism teaches there can be no real miracles, so the miracles of the Bible are only there to tell a story or portray a moral.

As a result even in the denominational church there are those who no longer believe in the literal resurrection of Jesus, or the virgin birth. Some parts of the church have rejected the age old doctrine of marriage and accepted alternatives. Marriage has historically always been between a man and a woman, and in God's eyes always will be.

Paul spoke of these problems that would arise...

1 Timothy 4:1-3 *"Now the Spirit expressly says that in latter times some will depart from the faith, giving heed to deceiving spirits and doctrines of demons, ² speaking lies in hypocrisy, having their own conscience seared with a hot iron, ³ forbidding to marry, and commanding to abstain from foods which God created to be received with thanksgiving by those who believe and know the truth."*

In Revelation we read of a religious system that God describes as a harlot. This is the system that will exist at the end, and it will prostitute the truth. It is probable this religious system may be a result of the ecumenical efforts to merge all religions into one. There has been much effort put into merging faiths, including interfaith conferences and prayer. One of the prime movements in this has been the World Council of Churches.

At this great ecumenical gathering, the World Council of Churches (WCC) in Vancouver, Canada on July 24–August 10, 1983 the following revealing comments were appended to the official "Guide":

*"In the end, the great religious communities will not disappear. No one will have the upper hand. Jews will remain Jews; Muslims will remain Muslims; and those belonging to the great Oriental religions will remain Hindus, Buddhists, and Taoists. Africa will express its own view of the world; China will retain her heritage. As before, people will continue to travel from the East to the West, from the North to the South, **and to abide in the Kingdom of God without, in consequence, having first become Christians like us [!]."***

The leaders of many mainline denominations, particularly the Anglican and Catholic churches have joined together to pray as though their God were the same as those of other faiths. Certainly not all the members of these churches would agree with this, but the trend is alarming.

There is a big difference between having respect for one another, and living in peace, and actually embracing other religions.

This final religious system will be used by the Anti-Christ to gain power, and will support him, though he will ultimately turn on this system as he will then demand all the worship himself.

Such things are clearly predicted in the Bible...

2 Timothy 4:1-4 *"I charge you therefore before God and the Lord Jesus Christ, who will judge the living and the dead at His appearing and His kingdom:* ² *Preach the word! Be ready in season and out of season. Convince, rebuke, exhort, with all long suffering and teaching.* ³ *For the time will come when they will not endure sound doctrine, but according to their own desires, because they have itching ears, they will heap up for themselves teachers;* ⁴ *and they will turn their ears away from the truth, and be turned aside to fables."*

A Counterfeit Trinity

The devil is a counterfeiter, and in the end times will counterfeit the Holy trinity. His desire to be God himself, and his hatred of the true God will be his motivation.

The Anti-Christ will be a false Christ, Satan as a false God the Father, and the false prophet as a false Holy Spirit. The Anti-Christ will, according to Revelation, have a fatal wound but live, thus mimicking the resurrection of Jesus.

The Anti-Christ is linked with the false prophet who will be his chief promoter.

Revelation 13:11-14 *"Another beast coming up out of the earth and he had two horns like a lamb and spoke like a dragon.* ¹² *And he exercises all the authority of the first beast in his presence, and causes the earth and those who dwell in it to worship the first beast, whose deadly wound was healed.* ¹³ *He performs great signs, so that he even makes fire come down from heaven on the earth in the sight of men.* ¹⁴ *And he deceives those who dwell on the earth by those signs which he was granted to do in the sight of the beast, telling those who dwell on the earth to make an image to the beast who was wounded by the sword and lived."*

One TOUCHSTONE that will protect you from deception

If Adam and Eve had simply trusted what God said, even if they did not fully understand why He said it, they would never have fallen into sin.

Trust in God's word is so important.

Jesus said in Matthew 24:35... *"Heaven and earth will pass away, but My words will by no means pass away."*

And Isaiah 40:8... *"The grass withers, the flower fades, But the word of our God stands forever."*

Only a love of the truth will protect us in the days in which we live and from what is to come. The Bible is the revelation of God's truth, and any belief or system stands or falls by comparison to God's word, the truth.

It is very sad that part of the end time deception will involve the church. In 2 Thessalonians 2:1-4 we read...

"Now, brethren, concerning the coming of our Lord Jesus Christ and our gathering together to Him, we ask you, ² not to be soon shaken in mind or troubled either by spirit or by word or by letter, as if from us, as though the day of Christ had come. ³ Let no one deceive you by any means; for that Day will not come unless the falling away comes first, and the man of sin is revealed, the son of perdition, ⁴ who opposes and exalts himself above all that is called God or that is worshiped, so that he sits as God in the temple of God, showing himself that he is God."

The word apostasy means "falling away". It is true of our society that there has been a falling away as belief in the major doctrines of the Bible is much lower than even 25 years ago. This falling away has even affected mainline denominations.

The greatest investment we can make is to get to know the Bible's message and to act upon it. Only a love of the truth will protect us from the deceptions of the last days.

What have we learned in this chapter...

- The word of God is the foundation for truth

- Many deceivers will come

- Occult practices are dangerous

"All other Books are of little importance in comparison with the Holy Scriptures"

Alexander Cruden

An Easy Guide To The End Times

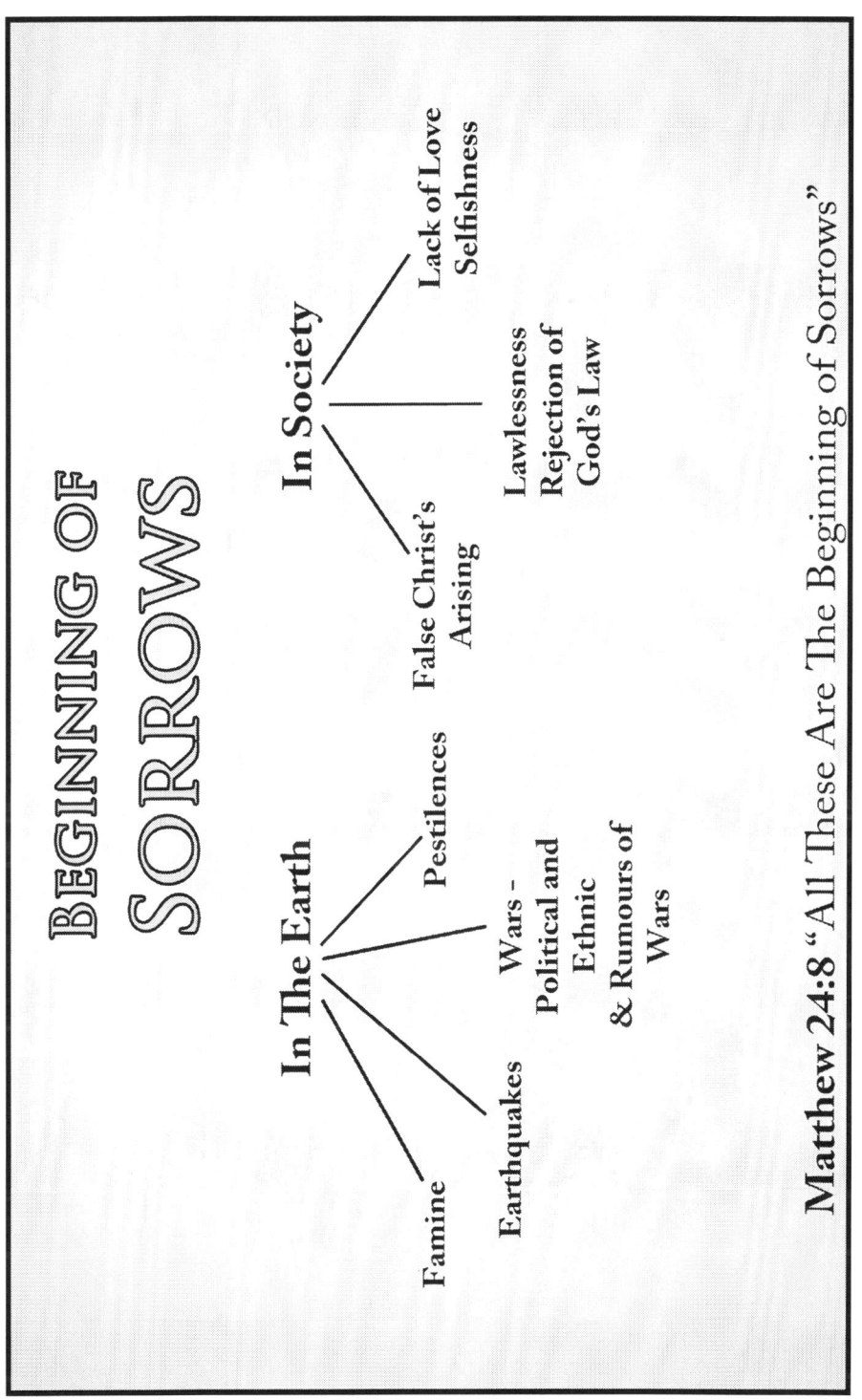

BEGINNING OF SORROWS

In The Earth
- Famine
- Earthquakes
- Wars – Political and Ethnic & Rumours of Wars
- Pestilences

In Society
- False Christ's Arising
- Lawlessness Rejection of God's Law
- Lack of Love Selfishness

Matthew 24:8 "All These Are The Beginning of Sorrows"

CHAPTER 9

The Beginning of Sorrows

The term "beginning of sorrows" is used a number of times in relation to the second coming of Jesus. In Jesus' discourse on the signs of His return He uses this term.

Matthew 24:4-8 *"And Jesus answered and said to them: 'Take heed that no one deceives you. ⁵ For many will come in My name, saying, 'I am the Christ,' and will deceive many. ⁶ And you will hear of wars and rumours of wars. See that you are not troubled; for all these things must come to pass, but the end is not yet.⁷ For nation will rise against nation, and kingdom against kingdom. And there will be famines, pestilences, and earthquakes in various places. ⁸ All these are the beginning of sorrows.' "*

Jesus lists five signs that mark the beginning of the labour pains.

1. **False Christs.** This has been fulfilled in history many times. The Jews have had many false Messiahs arise. It is true of our day also. There are many Gurus who consider themselves Christs, and many follow them. The Beetles were among the first to get involved with Indian Gurus, now it has become fashionable, and the associated new age teachings are commonplace.

2. **Wars and rumours of wars.** The world has seen so many wars. Since the Second World War more people have been killed in other wars than were killed then. Two world wars as kingdom rose against kingdom. There are many wars taking place in the world today, and rumours abound as Iran, Russia and other nations share a hatred for Israel.

3. **Famines.** Despite there being enough food to feed everyone there

continues to be desperate famines that kill so many. Sadly politics often supersede hurting people, and weapons seem greater priority than food. Increasingly erratic weather patterns exacerbate the situation.

4. **Pestilences.** Disease follows famines and disasters. AIDS is a modern pestilence that has ravaged huge parts of the population in some African countries leaving many orphans. With the rise in the knowledge of biological warfare there may be worse to come if nations start to employ them overt or covert warfare. The western world seems also to be ravaged by heart disease and cancer, partly through lifestyle choices.

5. **Earthquakes** seem commonplace now and are increasing in intensity particularly in the last fifty to one hundred years.

1 Thessalonians 5:1-3 uses similar language... *"But concerning the times and the seasons, brethren, you have no need that I should write to you.^{2} For you yourselves know perfectly that the day of the Lord so comes as a thief in the night. ^{3} For when they say, "Peace and safety!" then sudden destruction comes upon them, as labour pains upon a pregnant woman. And they shall not escape."*

Again we see labour pains all around our world today. In this reference we see that many will be saying peace and safety. This is certainly true of past judgements. At the time of Jeremiah and Ezekiel God warned the people of certain judgement coming. At the time there were many false prophets proclaiming peace and safety. Despite all their positive words, Israel had to experience one of the worst times of their history. It would have been better for them if they had listened to the true prophets. It is exactly the same today.

When Noah entered the ark no one wanted to join him except his own family, despite the fact Noah was a preacher of righteousness. The people of the time were warned, but obviously believed words of peace and safety rather than the truth.

When Lot left Sodom the rest of the city were not perturbed. They were not convinced the city would be judged for its great evil.

When Jeremiah and Ezekiel warned of the destruction of Jerusalem the people listened to the other prophets who predicted peace and safety.

However, destruction did come just as they said it would.

Today many are talking of times of peace and safety. Few are warning that there is a coming day of recompense for the wickedness of the world, and its rejection of God and His word. Regardless of their words of peace, a day of recompense is coming soon!

Romans 8:19-22 *"For the earnest expectation of the creation eagerly waits for the revealing of the sons of God. ²⁰ For the creation was subjected to futility, not willingly, but because of Him who subjected it in hope; ²¹ because the creation itself also will be delivered from the bondage of corruption into the glorious liberty of the children of God. ²² For we know that the whole creation groans and labours with birth pangs together until now."*

In the letter to the Romans we see the same term. This shows that the earth itself is groaning and waiting for that day when the "sons of God" are revealed. That is the day when we, as saints return with the Lord Jesus, and the power of the curse sin brought is finally reversed.

The things we are seeing in our day are surely the beginning of sorrows. Given the fact that Israel is in the land, the last world empire is arising, the nations surrounding Israel are vehemently opposed to them and other collaborating signs as we have discussed, there is little doubt that we are very near the end of the age.

Matthew 24:12 *"And because lawlessness will abound, the love of many will grow cold."*

Jesus also warned that in the stress and difficulties of the last days the love of many would grow cold. This is further elaborated by Paul's letter to Timothy...

2 Timothy 3:1-4 *"But know this, that in the last days perilous times shall come. ² For men shall be lovers of their own selves, covetous, boasters, proud, blasphemers, disobedient to parents, unthankful, unholy, ³ without natural affection, trucebreakers, false accusers, incontinent, fierce, despisers of those that are good,⁴ traitors, heady, highminded, lovers of pleasures more than lovers of God."*

"The BIBLE is the Constitution of Christianity"

Billy Graham

CHAPTER 10

What to do

All that you have read in this book points to one clear and certain truth... that there is a God. He has his hand on history, and we all need to be ready to meet with Him on the day of reckoning which will shortly be with us.

Becoming a Christian is the most important step in life. Life on earth is so short. Compared to eternity it is but a brief moment. We may feel invincible, but the years pass quickly by. Yet while our bodies will die every one of us will live for eternity! While there are those that believe we will just cease to be, they will be dead only seconds before they realize they were wrong.

It is during our time on earth that we have the opportunity to make peace with God. All the things we are seeing globally today point to this world rapidly coming to the end of its present state. The world is being shaken, until only that which cannot be shaken remains - all that is built on God's word.

God has gone to extreme lengths to make it possible for each one of us to be saved from the power of sin, and to receive eternal life with Him. He cares for you and me, and wants us to come to Him. He made plans so all could be with Him forever in peace, joy, wholeness, health and everlasting prosperity.

He wishes all to be saved and come to know Him, but not all will. Some will persistently resist His love and truth. But please know this; His plan has made room for you to be saved.

Satan's end is in the lake of fire (Revelation 19:20). He wants to drag as many humans with him as possible, and has gone to extreme lengths to slander God's word and stop people believing the truth.

The Problem...

We are each born into sin. Sin has I in the middle, and it is when we run our own lives, instead of looking to the Lord Jesus to be the Lord of all, that there is a big problem. The Bible terms this as sin – wilful rebellion against the Lordship of God in our lives.

The Ten Commandments picture God's standards. All of us have broken them, maybe only in small ways, yet they still remain broken.

Jesus said the greatest commandment is to love the Lord with all our heart, soul and strength. We have all broken this. Therefore because God is holy He cannot allow sin in His presence. Sin is not just a bad habit; it is a deeply interwoven part of man's nature. Even with all the laws and moral standards we have applied, somehow sin keeps producing evil in various forms across the earth.

Ever since Adam and Eve, sin has been passed down to every succeeding generation as an inheritance that no one can escape. Therefore, this inherited sin is fully part of every human's nature.

That is why we need laws, because they help keep order and stop man completely giving in to the evil side of his nature. Compared to God's amazing holiness we are all sinners. Even the most righteous person when compared to the holiness of God is revealed to be a sinner. It isn't until we experience the purity and holiness of God that we fully realize how unclean and "contaminated" by sin we are.

Look at this commandment Jesus spoke about:

Matthew 22:37 *"You shall love the LORD your God with all your heart, with all your soul, and with all your strength."*

Not one of us has fully obeyed this. No; we are far short of God's glory.

Romans 3:23 *"For all have sinned and fall short of the glory of God,"*

The Result

Romans 6:23 *"For the wages of sin is death, but the gift of God is eternal life in Christ Jesus our Lord."*

So the Bible states clearly that the result of sin is death. This death is firstly spiritual. Our spirits are dead to God because of sin. The spirit is the part of us made to fellowship with God.

Jesus said in John 4:24... *"God is Spirit, and those who worship Him must worship in spirit and truth."*

Only when we are forgiven of our sins and made whole through God's forgiveness and reconciliation can we then begin to really know God.

Sin's effect begins within, in our spirit, and then affects soul, (our will and emotions) and our body, which will eventually die. Sin's effect is terminal and will result in eternal separation from God.

In Ephesians 2:1 Christians are reminded... *"And you He made alive, who were dead in trespasses and sins."*

Sin is a terminal condition. It has brought death, cut us off from God, and has only one cure.

None of our own religiosity, good works or efforts can make us good enough. To get right with God and become a Christian, we have to come to the place we recognise that we are sinners, that we have failed and need God's forgiveness.

God's Remedy

The Bible explains there was only one thing that could pay for the death sin brought about; life itself. That is why there was animal sacrifice in the Old Testament. Blood had to be shed to pay for the death brought about by sin with the life of another.

Leviticus 17:11 *"For the life of the flesh is in the blood, and I have given it to you upon the altar to make atonement for your souls; for it is the blood that makes atonement for the soul."*

However...

The blood of animals was not in itself enough. God asked for this sacrifice for a number of reasons.

It pointed forward to the blood sacrifice Jesus would make centuries later.

It reminded us of the grave consequences of our sin.

It showed that sin had a very serious cost.

Therefore...

God in His love sent Jesus, God the Son to be the final sacrifice, to deal with sin in a once for all sacrifice. [

Hebrews 9:28 tells us..."*So Christ was offered once to bear the sins of many...*"

Jesus' sacrifice was different because...

1. He was sinless; no one else in history could make this claim. He did no evil. 1Peter 1:18-19 says...

    "*For as much as ye know that ye were not redeemed with corruptible things, as silver and gold, from your vain conversation received by tradition from your fathers; [19] But with the precious blood of Christ, as of a lamb without blemish and without spot.*"

2. He took on the nature of man (whilst still being God) so He could relate to us, and suffer in our place.

Jesus, therefore, became the sinless spotless sacrificial lamb for us.

When Jesus died on the cross in Jerusalem ALL our sin and guilt was laid on and imputed to Him. In His death, His broken body and shed blood paid the price for us to be forgiven and healed so we could be restored to full peace and harmony in a relationship with God.

John 3:16-17 "*For God so loved the world that He gave His only begotten Son, that whoever believes in Him should not perish but have everlasting life.[17]For God did not send His Son into the world to condemn the world, but that the world through Him might be saved.*"

If we put our faith in Jesus' sacrifice the Bible makes it clear that we can be forgiven, and start a new life. Life that is EVERLASTING, ETERNAL and can never be destroyed or lost. Jesus is the only way; because our own works can never achieve what is necessary.

Jesus told Nicodemas in John 3:3... *"Most assuredly, I say to you, unless one is born of water and the Spirit, he cannot enter the kingdom of God."*

We all need to be born a second time. The first time is our natural birth; the second is a spiritual birth.

How does this happen?

Step 1

Believe in the Lord Jesus Christ.

Firstly we need to recognise that Jesus Christ alone has the power to forgive and restore us. He is God the son, who died for us, and rose victorious over sin, Satan and death, on the third day.

Step 2

Recognise that we are sinners. When we understand that we are sinners, we need to repent. To repent means to make a decision to turn away from sin and towards God, to say sorry to Him. We need to ask His forgiveness and then to commit to change with His help.

Step 3

Being a Christian also means that you will have God living on the very inside of our person. Having been forgiven we invite God to come into our lives, not only as the forgiver of our sin, and our healer, but also as our Lord, our friend, our counsellor and ever present helper.

Pray with me now if you would like to be forgiven and receive eternal life

Say this prayer out loud, think carefully about every word and be sincere.

Father I come to You in Jesus' name. I believe that Jesus is the Son of God, that He died in my place, bearing my sin, paying for me with His body and blood on the Cross, and that He rose from the dead victorious.

I am truly sorry for everything I have done that is offensive to You. Please help me from this point, as I turn now from all sin to live for Your glory. Please forgive me.

Thank you for Your forgiveness Lord. I also thank You that because I have believed the good news of Jesus Christ with all my heart I now have eternal life!

I invite You Lord to fully enter my life. To be my Lord. To lead me, and to teach me all I need to know in the future. Fill me with Your Holy Spirit and give me power to be a good witness for You.

I ask all these things Father, in the Name of Your dear Son, Jesus Christ.

If you have prayed this prayer, please e-mail us or write and let us know. We would like to send you a free booklet to help you.

Some *very* Important Steps to take

- Tell someone what you have done

- Jesus said *"Whosoever therefore shall confess me before men, him will I confess also before my Father which is in heaven."* (Matthew 10:32)

- Pray daily. Pray to the Father in Jesus' name. Pray with reverence, but with openness. Be thankful, and share your needs with God, trusting Him to help as you pray. The Lord's Prayer is a good guide. Think about each part as you pray.

- Read the Bible daily. It will help you grow and mature as a Christian. Seek to not only read it but to apply it.

- Find a Bible believing church where you can learn, grow, and be a blessing to others. The church is God's plan for believers, you need to be there to receive from others, and so others can receive from you.

Some important verses, and remember; God always keeps His promises:-

Romans 10:9-11 *"That if you confess with your mouth the Lord Jesus and believe in your heart that God has raised Him from the dead, you will be saved.[10] For with the heart one believes unto righteousness, and with the mouth confession is made unto salvation.[11] For the Scripture says, "Whoever believes on Him will not be put to shame."*

2 Corinthians 5:17 *"Therefore, if anyone is in Christ, he is a new creation; old things have passed away; behold, all things have become new."*

It's true. YOU are a BRAND NEW PERSON NOW. Hallelujah!

If you have prayed and received Jesus Christ as your personal saviour, please fill out this form as a record of your commitment.

I _____ *prayed on* _____
and received Jesus Christ as my personal saviour. I repented of my sin, and handed the Lordship of my life to God. I am now a Christian.

Signed _____

Ignite Ministries

Jonathan and Deborah Fiddy are the founders and leaders of Ignite Ministries.

Ignite is the fulfilment of a vision that has been in our hearts for many years. We believe now is the right time to launch forth and hold public meetings as God leads, and be in partnership with local churches where possible. The need is so great, and so many have never heard the Gospel of Jesus Christ, or seen the demonstration of the power of the Holy Spirit.

The Gospel of Jesus Christ has been entrusted to us who believe, and we have been given the Great Commission of sharing this good news. We live in a day when the gospel has been minimised, watered down and in some cases forgotten in a sea of political correctness.

Thank God we have good news of hope and healing to share!

We pray fervently for a national awakening, but in the meantime we need to work tirelessly to share the good news with as many as possible. The time is short as we see a rising tide of political and financial turmoil, and increasing natural disasters. Our response must be, to be fervent in getting the message out. We are grateful to our partners - your prayers and in some cases financial support make it possible for us to go out. Thank you!

Website: igniteministries.co.uk   **Phone:** 01834 871975

Made in the USA
Charleston, SC
27 December 2012